Schöningh

EinFach
Englisch
Unterrichtsmodell

Exploring Australian Identities

Short Stories of the Australian Experience

Edited by
Frauke Matz
Michael Rogge

Series Editor:
Hans Kröger

Audio-CD
Einzelarbeit
Partnerarbeit
Gruppenarbeit
Unterrichtsgespräch
Schreibauftrag
Hausaufgabe
filmische Präsentation
Projekt, offene Aufgabe
kreative Aufgabe
szenisches Spiel, Rollenspiel

Vorwort

Der Titel der Reihe **EinFach Englisch** verdeutlicht Zielsetzung und Programm zugleich. Einerseits soll Schülerinnen und Schülern auf einfache Art und Weise der Zugang zu klassischen, aber auch neuen literarischen Werken und Filmen ermöglicht werden, andererseits sollen Lehrerinnen und Lehrern in der Praxis erprobte Unterrichtsmodelle angeboten werden, die die wichtigsten methodisch-didaktischen Ansätze ihres Faches Englisch abdecken. Dabei sind die Modelle direkt, ohne langes Einlesen einsetzbar und stellen Unterrichtsarbeit konkret vor. Als besonders hilfreich für die Praxis haben sich dabei folgende Aspekte erwiesen, die für die Gestaltung der Reihe wesentlich sind:

- Überblick über **Figurenkonstellation**, ggf. **Filmszenen** und **Inhalt**
- **Klausuren** mit **Erwartungshorizont**
- **Arbeitsblätter, Tafelbilder** und **Leitfragen** für den Unterricht
- **Piktogramme** als Hinweise auf **Unterrichts-** und **Arbeitsformen**

Das Prinzip der „**Components**" ermöglicht darüber hinaus den variablen Einsatz der Modelle in unterschiedlich konzipierten Unterrichtsreihen. Dabei stehen Machbarkeit und Praxisnähe stets im Vordergrund.

Das vorliegende Modell bezieht sich auf folgende Textausgabe: *Short Stories of the Australian Experience*, edited by Thomas Rau, Diesterweg, Braunschweig 2010

Sprachliche Betreuung: Alexandra Rieb

www.schoeningh-schulbuch.de
Schöningh Verlag, Jühenplatz 1–3, 33098 Paderborn

Druck 5 4 3 2 1 / Jahr 2015 14 13 12 11
Die letzte Zahl bezeichnet das Jahr dieses Druckes.

Umschlaggestaltung: Jennifer Kirchhof
Druck und Bindung: westermann druck GmbH, Braunschweig

ISBN 978-3-14-041184-4

Getting started

DOES AUSTRALIA NEED A NATIONAL IDENTITY?

Australia needs sudden shocks of reorientation within its society that will divorce it from the largely irrelevant problems of the British, make it possible to speed necessary changes and to develop some sense of identity, some public feeling of being a people who can be described – even if incorrectly – as such-and-such a nation, and act at times if it were so. Australians are anonymous, featureless, nothing-men. This modest anonymity reveals itself in the argument that Australia does not run to the kind of person we could turn into a president.

Donald Horne (1964), Australian writer

Being Australian is not simply about the pleasure of the past and the excitement of the future ... It is not just about that funny feeling a citizen might get when the Australian flag is raised at the Olympics. Being Australian also encompasses feelings, ideas and emotions that vary from joy to shame, guilt to confession, hatred to love. Yet, in most national narratives these feelings of anxiety are erased or represented in favour of the pleasurable aspects of national identity. Finding pleasure in being Australian is valuable, however, exploring and explaining the anxiety and fear that lie at the heart of the idea of being Australian is also important.

Catriona Elder, Being Australian (2007), lecturer in the department of Sociology at the University of Sydney

We must be the only country in the world that marks its national day not by celebrating its identity, but by questioning it.

Ken Boundy, Managing Director of the Australian Tourist Commission

Exploring Australian Identities

Component 2: Continued

Component 3: Aboriginal identities 66

Component 4: Multicultural identity 86

Die Textsammlung *Short Stories of the Australian Experience*

1. Price Warung (William Astley): *How Muster-Master Stoneman Earned His Breakfast* (1892)

Diese Kurzgeschichte spielt im 19. Jahrhundert im Van-Diemens-Land, dem heutigen Tasmanien, und steht exemplarisch für das Leben britischer Sträflinge in den australischen Strafgefangenenkolonien.

Es geht einerseits um den Leiter einer dieser australischen Strafkolonien, Stoneman, und andererseits um den Strafgefangenen Glancy. Glancy, der eigentlich wegen des Diebstahls eines seidenen Taschentuches verhaftet und zu einer sieben Jahre langen Haftstrafe verurteilt wurde, sitzt nun wegen Mordes ein. Während Glancy im Rahmen seiner Strafe an einem Straßenbau beteiligt war, ermordete er einen Aufseher, den gewalttätigen James Jones. Die Geschichte beginnt am Vorabend von Glancys Hinrichtung und erstreckt sich über den Zeitraum von etwa 16 Stunden.

An diesem Septemberabend gegen 17 Uhr besucht Kaplan Ford den Gefangenen, um ihm den letzten Beistand zu leisten. Glancy beobachtet aber die Vorbereitungen für seine Hinrichtung, die am nächsten Morgen um 9 Uhr stattfinden soll, und schickt den Kaplan fort. Dieser verspricht, um 5 Uhr morgens wiederzukommen.

Um 22 Uhr abends wechselt die Wache und Glancy, der nur an den Beinen gefesselt ist, ermordet den Wächter mit dessen eigenem Bajonett und hebt mithilfe dieses Bajonetts im Verlauf der nächsten Stunden einen Tunnel aus, um zu entkommen. Seine Flucht wird erst bei der Wachablösung um 5 Uhr morgens bemerkt. Nun beginnt die Suche nach dem Strafgefangenen unter der Leitung Stonemans.

Bevor sie jedoch Glancy aufspüren können, kehrt dieser selbstständig zu dem Gefängnis zurück und stellt sich. Auf die Frage, warum er überhaupt ausgebrochen sei, erwidert Glancy, er habe auf Jones' Grab spucken wollen.

Stoneman verurteilt Glancy um halb sieben für den Ausbruch zu einer Strafe von hundert Peitschenhieben, die um 7 Uhr ausgeführt wird. Eine halbe Stunde später wird Glancy zurück in seine Zelle gebracht, in der um 8 Uhr der Henker Johnson erscheint und als zusätzliche Bestrafung Salz in die frischen Wunden des Strafgefangenen streut.

Als um 8.45 Uhr Sheriff Rope dazukommt, herrscht Unschlüssigkeit darüber, ob die für 9 Uhr angesetzte Hinrichtung auch stattfinden soll. Stoneman erwidert darauf jedoch, dass die Lage eindeutig sei: Glancy müsse pünktlich hingerichtet und erst danach für die letzte Straftat zur Rechenschaft gezogen werden. Glancy wird schließlich wenige Minuten später gehängt und um Viertel nach zehn begraben.

Im Anschluss daran verabschiedet sich Stoneman vom Sheriff, um zu frühstücken.

2. Henry Lawson: *The Drover's Wife* (1892)

Die Frau des Viehtreibers ist mit ihren vier Kindern und ihrem Hund namens Alligator allein auf der Farm im australischen Hinterland, ihr Mann ist mit einer Schafsherde seit längerer Zeit unterwegs.

Während des Tages sieht eines der Kinder eine Schlange, die unter dem Haus verschwindet. Der Hund kann die Schlange nicht erwischen und die Frau muss nun fürchten, dass die Schlange jederzeit im Hause auftauchen und jemanden aus der Familie beißen könnte.

Die Frau sorgt dafür, dass die Kinder während der folgenden Nacht auf dem Küchentisch schlafen und somit für das Tier nicht erreichbar sind. Sie selbst versucht, sich wach zu halten, und reflektiert über ihr einsames Leben im australischen Busch, über ihre Ehe und die Schwierigkeiten, die ihr dieses Leben bereits bereitet hat. Schließlich denkt sie darüber nach, dass

sie diese Art zu leben zunächst zwar verabscheute, sich aber nun ein anderes Leben nicht mehr vorstellen könnte.
Am frühen Morgen findet der Hund endlich die Schlange und die Frau kann sie töten.

3. Katharine Susannah Prichard: *Marlene* (1938)
In dieser Kurzgeschichte besuchen die weiße Australierin Mrs Boyd, die sich um die Aborigines zu kümmern scheint, und die Engländerin Miss Cecily Allison, die ein Buch über die Aborigines schreibt, ein Camp für sogenannte *half-caste* Aborigines.
Sie suchen und fragen nach einem Mädchen im Teenager-Alter namens Mollie. Die Campbewohner versuchen immer wieder, von der Suche nach Mollie abzulenken, indem sie von anderen Bewohnern sowie über ihr eigenes Leben sprechen. Die Lebensbedingungen in dem Camp sind äußerst schwierig und auf die Frage, wie sie von den Aborigines selbst aufgenommen werden, wird deutlich, dass diese *half-caste* Aborigines weder von den Weißen noch von den Schwarzen akzeptiert oder gar als zugehörig gesehen werden, jedoch von den Schwarzen mit etwas mehr Respekt behandelt werden. Schließlich erscheint Mollie, jedoch zu Mrs Boyds Überraschung mit ihrem neugeborenen Kind, von dem Mrs Boyd nichts zu wissen schien.
Es stellt sich heraus, dass Mrs Boyd eine negative Einstellung zu den *half-caste* Aborigines hat und Mollie mit ihrem außerehelichen Baby ablehnt. Es wird zum Ende der Kurzgeschichte erwähnt, dass das Camp nur kurze Zeit nach Mrs Boyds Besuch verlegt wird.

4. Archie Weller: *Going Home* (1986)
Die 21-jährige Hauptfigur dieser Kurzgeschichte ist William Jakob Woodward, ein Aborigine mit einem weißen Vorfahren, der sich auf dem Weg zurück zu seiner Familie nach Guildford befindet, einem Vorort von Perth. Während der Autofahrt erinnert sich Billy an die vergangenen Jahre:
Im Alter von 16 Jahren ging Billy auf ein College in Perth, wo er bereits im ersten Jahr als guter Fußballspieler auffiel. Mit 18 spielte er mit großem Erfolg für das beste Team der Stadt und fühlte sich eher wie ein Weißer und nicht mehr wie ein Aborigine. Seine Familie besuchte er in dieser Zeit nie.
Er besteht nach seinem fünften Jahr am College und geht an das West Australian Institute of Technology, um dort Malerei weiterzustudieren. Er lässt sich sein langes Haar schneiden und beginnt, sich wie die Weißen zu kleiden und das Leben in Nachtclubs zu genießen. An einem Abend trifft er zufällig auf seine Tante Rose, schämt sich jedoch für sie, da sie sehr heruntergekommen aussieht, und kehrt ihr den Rücken zu.
Die Erzählung konzentriert sich nun wieder auf die Gegenwart: Während der Autofahrt nimmt Billy einen Aborigine namens Darcy Goodrich mit, der seine Familie kennt und ihm erzählt, dass Billys Vater, Teddy Woodward, bereits vor zwei Jahren bei einem Unfall ums Leben gekommen sei. Durch den Konsum von billigem Alkohol sei dieser erblindet und habe entsprechend den Lastwagen nicht gesehen, der ihn schließlich überfahren habe.
Billy fühlt sich unangenehm berührt und ihm wird bei dem Gedanken an seine Familie bewusst, dass er eigentlich zu diesen Menschen gehört.
Als er heimkommt, erkennt ihn zunächst niemand. Carlton, sein Bruder, und sein Cousin Rennie unterhalten sich schließlich mit ihm, seine Mutter scheint aber nicht auf ihn zu reagieren. Carlton und Rennie leihen sich Billys Auto und begehen einen Diebstahl, ohne dass Billy selbst davon weiß. Sein Bruder schenkt ihm eine Uhr zum Geburtstag, die Billy noch in derselben Nacht zum Verhängnis wird. Da er nicht schlafen kann, geht er spazieren und wird von der Polizei aufgegriffen und verhaftet. Die Uhr und die Tatsache, dass es sein Auto war, reichen den Polizisten als Beweis dafür, dass auch Billy mit dem Raub zu tun hat. Die Polizei ignoriert seinen Protest und betont, alle Woodwards seien gleich.

5. Tim Winton: *Neigbours* (1985)

In seiner Kurzgeschichte beschreibt Tim Winton die Situation eines jungen Ehepaares, das von einem ruhigen Vorort in ein Stadtviertel zieht, in dem viele europäische Einwanderer wohnen. Ihre direkten Nachbarn sind eine mazedonische Familie sowie ein polnischer Witwer. In den ersten Monaten empfindet das junge Paar die neue Wohnsituation als sehr störend und fremd. Sie beobachten ihre Nachbarn mit Argwohn und können ihre Eigenarten nicht nachvollziehen. Dies beruht jedoch auf Gegenseitigkeit, da auch die Nachbarn das Ehepaar als komisch empfinden: Beide stehen spät auf und während der Ehemann an seiner Doktorarbeit schreibt, geht seine Frau arbeiten. Als die junge Frau ungeplant schwanger wird, erschwert sich die Lebenssituation der beiden. Die Schwangerschaft spricht sich jedoch in der Nachbarschaft sehr schnell herum und das junge Paar trifft überall auf Freundlichkeit und Hilfsbereitschaft. Sie sind über die Anteilnahme erstaunt und fühlen sich zu ihrem eigenen Erstaunen im Verlauf der Schwangerschaft immer mehr in das Stadtviertel integriert.

Story	Setting	Protagonists	Plot
How Muster-Master Stoneman earned his breakfast pp. 10–24	Van Diemen's Land (Tasmania), Convict Colony, late 19th century	Muster-Master Stoneman, Convict Glancy	Convict Glancy escapes from prison after killing a warden, spits on the grave of a man he murdered, returns to prison and is executed.
The Drover's Wife pp. 27–39	Australian outback, late 19th century	The drover's wife, her children, a dog, a snake	A drover's wife protects her children from a snake.
Marlene pp. 43–58	Camp for so-called *half-caste* Aborigines	Mrs Boyd, a white Australian woman, Miss Cecily Allison, inhabitants of the camp, Mollie, a *half-caste* Aborigine	Mrs Boyd visits a camp for Aborigines because she is looking for a teenage girl called Mollie; Mollie appears with a newborn baby, to Mrs Boyd's surprise. The camp is moved elsewhere shortly afterwards.
Going Home pp. 60–78	Guildford and Perth, late 20th century	Billy, an Aborigine; his brother Carlton and cousin Rennie, Darcy Goodrich, also an Aborigine	Billy, a 21-year-old Aborigine returns home after having lived a successful life away from his family for five years. He gets arrested for a crime he didn't commit.
Neighbours pp. 82–87	An Australian city, late 20th century	A young married couple and their neighbours	A married couple moves into a neighbourhood where many European immigrants live. After initial prejudices they feel accepted in this new neighbourhood.

Konzeption des Unterrichtsmodells

Das Unterrichtsmodell bezieht sich auf insgesamt fünf Kurzgeschichten, die in der Textsammlung *Short Stories of the Australian Experience* (hrsg. von Thomas Rau) zusammengefasst sind.

Die Auswahl der Texte entspricht den fachbezogenen Hinweisen zum Zentralabitur 2012 in Niedersachsen, wo die genannten Texte dem erhöhten Anforderungsniveau entsprechen und den Themenfeldern „National identity and ethnic/cultural/language diversities", „Beliefs, values and norms in Western societies: Tradition and change" sowie dem Bereich „Individual and society" zugeordnet sind.

Die Texte ermöglichen einen vertieften Einblick in die kulturelle Pluralität und die Problematik der nationalen Identität Australiens, die nicht nur durch die koloniale Vergangenheit (vgl. hierzu ***Component 1*** und ***2*** mit den *short stories How Muster-Master-Stoneman Earned His Breakfast* und *The Drover's Wife*), sondern auch durch die Auseinandersetzung mit der indigenen Bevölkerung Australiens (hierzu ***Component 3*** mit den Kurzgeschichten *Marlene* und *Going Home*) und die Problematik heutiger Identitätsfindung in einer multikulturellen und plurilingualen Gesellschaft mit Einwanderern aus vielen unterschiedlichen Kulturkreisen (vgl. hierzu ***Component 4*** und die Kurzgeschichte *Neighbours*) gekennzeichnet ist.

Das Unterrichtsmodell will gerade durch die Kontrastierung der fünf Kurzgeschichten den Schülerinnen und Schülern intertextuelle Zugänge zur Thematik ermöglichen (vgl. Hallet 1998, 2002), die nicht nur zu einem vertieften Textverstehen und einer Auseinandersetzung mit den besonderen Merkmalen der *short story,* wie z. B. die Figurencharakterisierung, die Untersuchung der Handlungsstruktur oder weiterer Mittel der Textgestaltung beitragen sollen, sondern zugleich den Schülerinnen und Schülern durch Perspektivwechsel und Perspektivenkoordination sowohl vertiefte Einblicke in die Vielschichtigkeit australischer Gesellschaft (Innenperspektive) als auch den kritischen Blick auf die Problematik nationaler Identitätsfindung in einer postkolonialen Gesellschaft (Außenperspektive) ermöglichen.
Dabei erlaubt der zeitliche Rahmen der Kurzgeschichten, die von der Frühphase des kolonialen Australiens als *penal colony* über die Lebenserfahrungen weißer Siedler und den problematischen Umgang mit den Aborigines und deren Jahrtausende alten kulturellen Vergangenheit bis hin zur heutigen Diskussion über die Identität Australiens als klassischem Einwanderungsland reichen, verschiedene Traditionen und Wertesysteme deutlich werden zu lassen und den allmählichen Wandel der australischen Gesellschaft zu verdeutlichen. Um allerdings die Merkmale und Besonderheiten australischer Gesellschaft sowie die spezifischen erzählerischen Aspekte der verschiedenen *short stories* zu kontrastieren, bedarf es einer entsprechenden Kontextualisierung und Didaktisierung der vorliegenden Texte. Dazu soll das vorliegende Unterrichtsmodell beitragen, indem es die vorliegenden Texte in den unterrichtlichen Zusammenhang stellt und die narrative Besonderheiten für Schülerinnen und Schüler herausstellt und nutzbar macht.

Klausuren

Klausur 1 kann nach der Erarbeitung von *Component 3* gestellt werden, die Erarbeitung von *Component 1* und *2* ist nicht erforderlich, wird aber als sinnvoll erachtet. Es ist möglich, diese Klausur auch in einem Grundkurs zu stellen.
Im Gegensatz dazu ist die Erarbeitung aller *Components* für die **Klausur 2** notwendig, da sie den Abschluss der Unterrichtsreihe bildet. Aufgrund des geforderten umfangreichen Kontextwissens ist diese Klausur gegebenenfalls eher für einen Leistungskurs geeignet.

Thea Astley: Heart is where the home is (excerpt)

"Listen, lady," the sergeant said, his face congested with the suppressed need to punch this cheeky sheilah right down her own hallway, "that's not what they tell me at the camp."
"What's not what they tell you?"
"She's got a kid all right. She's hiding it some place."
George's eyes, she saw, were strained with affection and concern. *Come up,* her own eyes begged him. *Come up.* "Sergeant," she said, "I have known Nelly since she was a young girl. She's helped out here for the last four years. Do you think I wouldn't know if she had a child? Do you? But you're free to search the house, if you want, and the grounds. You're thirsting for it, aren't you, warrant or not?"
The men shoved roughly past her at that, flattening Nelly Mumbler against the wall, and creaked down the hallway, into bedrooms and parlor and out into the kitchen. Cupboard doors crashed open. There was a banging of washhouse door.
George came up the steps and took his wife's arm, steering her and Nelly to the back of the house and putting them behind him as he watched the police come in from the yard. "Satisfied?"
"No, we're not, mate," the sergeant replied nastily. "Not one bloody bit."
Their powerful bodies crowded the kitchen out. They watched contemptuously as Nelly crept back to the sink, her body tensed with fright. "We don't believe you, missus," the sergeant said. "Not you or your hubby. There'll be real trouble for both of you when we catch you out." Mag held herself braced against infant squawls that might expose them at any minute. She made herself busy stoking the stove. "Righto," George said, pressing her arm and looking sharp and hard at the other men. "You've had your look. Now would you mind leaving. We've all got work to get on with." The sergeant was sulky. He scraped his boots about and kept glancing around the kitchen and out the door into the back garden.
The Laffeys' small girl was getting under his feet and pulling at his trouser legs, driving him crazy.
"All right," he agreed reluctantly. "All right." He gave one last stare at Nelly's back. "Fuckin' boongs," he said, deliberately trying to offend that stuck-up Mrs Laffey. "More trouble than they're worth. And that's bloody nothing."
The two women remained rooted in the kitchen while George went back up the track to his spadework. The sound of the horses died away.
At the sink Nelly kept washing and washing, her eyes never leaving the suds, the dishmop, the plate she endlessly scoured. Even after the thud of hoof faded beyond the ridge, even after that. And even after Mag Laffey took a cloth and began wiping the dishes and stacking them in the cupboard, even after that.
Mag saw her husband come round the side of the house, toss his hat on an outside peg and sit on the top step to ease his earth-stuck clobbers of boots off. Nelly's stiffly curved back asked question upon question. Her long brown fingers asked. Her turned-away face asked. When her baby toddled back into the kitchen, taken down from the bedroom ceiling manhole where George had hidden him with a lolly to suck, Nelly stayed glued to that sink washing that one plate. "Come on, Nelly," Mag said softly. "What's the matter? We've beaten them, haven't we?" George had picked up the small black boy and his daughter and was bouncing a child on each knee, waggling his head lovingly between them both while small hands pawed his face.
Infinitely slowly, Nelly turned from the sink, her fingers dripping soap and water. She looked at George Laffey cuddling a white baby and a black but she couldn't smile. "Come next time," she said, hopeless. "Come next time." George and his wife looked at her with terrible pity. They knew this as well. They knew. "And we'll do the same next time," Mag Laffey stated. "You don't have to worry."

congested here: red with anger, flushed
sheilah (*AustrE sl.*) young woman
strained *gespannt*
warrant here: offical permission to search the house
parlor sitting room
hubby (*infml.*) husband
to hold oneself braced against sth. here: to be prepared for sth. unpleasant
infant squawl loud crying of a baby
sulky silent and bad-tempered
reluctantly unwilling
boong (*AustrE sl.*) Aborigine
to remain rooted to stay exactly where you are
to scour to rub clean
thud dull sound
clobbers of boots (*AustrE sl.*) big boots

Then George Laffey said, "You come live here, Nelly. You come all time, eh?" His wife nodded at each word. Nodded and smiled and cried a bit. "You and Charley, eh?"

Nelly opened her mouth and wailed. *What is it!* they kept asking. *What's the matter! Wouldn't you like that!* They told her she could have the old store shed down by the river. They'd put a stove in and make it proper. Nelly kept crying, her dark eyes an unending fountain, and at last George became exasperated.

"You've got no choice, Nelly, he said, dropping the baby pidgin he had never liked anyway. "You've got no choice. If you come here we can keep an eye on Charley. If you don't, the government men will take him away.

You don't want that, do you? Why don't you want to come?" "Don't want to leave my family," she sobbed. "Don't want."

"God love us," George cried from the depths of his understanding, "God love us, they're only a mile up the river." He could feel his wife's fingers warning on his arm. "You can see them whenever you want."

"It's not same," Nelly insisted and sobbed. "Not same."

George thought he understood. He said, "You want Jackie, then. You want your husband to come along too, work in the garden maybe? Is that it?"

He put the baby into her arms and the two of them rocked somberly before him. He still hadn't understood.

The old men old women uncles aunts cousins brothers sisters tin humpies bottles dogs dirty blankets tobacco handouts fights river trees all the tribe's remnants and wretchedness, destruction and misery.

Her second skin now. "Not same," she whispered. And she cried them centuries of tribal dream in those two words. "Not same."

humpy native Australian hut
handout free gift

Thea Astley (1987). It's Raining in Mango: Pictures from a family Album. Camberwell: Penguin

Assignments

1. Describe the incident, which takes place in George and Mag Laffey's house, and explain the situation Nelly Mumbler appears to be in. (Comprehension)
2. Analyse how both the Laffeys and Nelly are portrayed in this situation and what the text reveals about their relationship. Take the narrator's language into consideration and pay special attention to the story's title. (Analysis)
3. Choose one of the following two tasks:

   a) Based on your knowledge about the Stolen Generation, comment on Nelly's situation as described in the story and discuss your views on this treatment of the Aboriginal people of Australia. (Evaluation: Comment)

   or

   b) After having calmed down, Nelly reflects on her thoughts and feelings during the incident and concerning George's offer. She writes a letter expressing her emotions to her husband and in order to weigh the arguments for and against accepting George's offer. Write this letter, expressing Nelly's thoughts especially on her treatment as an Aborigine by white people. (Creative task)

Erwartungshorizont zu Klausur 1

Zu 1: George and Mag Laffey are a white Australian married couple who have a small daughter and live at close distance to an Aborigines' camp. On the day the story takes place, the police has been informed by Aborigines in the nearby camp that Nelly Mumbler, also an Aborigine, is allegedly hiding at the Life's together with her daughter.

George Laffey tells the sergeant that Nelly has helped out in their household for the last four years and claims that he does not know where she is and that she certainly does not have a child.

However, Nelly and her child are in fact hiding in their house during the search, but the police fail to discover them. When the police is finally gone, Nelly is still very scared and already fears the next time the police will come and search for her.

George makes Nelly an offer: She and her little boy Charley should move out of the camp and live closer to the Laffeys. Nelly declines this offer, however, as she does not want to leave her family. George misinterprets her crying and extends the offer to Nelly's husband Jackie, who would be allowed to stay with them, too, and work for them. But Nelly cries even more and says that it would still not be the same.

Judging from this situation and the date of the short stories' publication, it may be inferred that the story takes place during the time of the so-called 'stolen generation'. Nelly is not allowed to have a child, as she is an Aborigine and, hence, should not procreate. The intention was to let the Aborigines slowly die out in restricting the birth rate. Their existing children were to be taken away and educated in camps under white Christian principles in order to mainly become servants to white families.

It is obvious that someone has denunciated Nelly and told the police that she has a child, which puts Nelly in a desperate situation: she cannot live in her camp with her husband anymore, but has to stay hidden away from her family in order to be with Charley and protect him.

Zu 2: Although the Laffeys are a white family, they don't seem to have any reservations towards Aboriginal people. The fact that they are indeed hiding Nelly and her son from the police and thereby putting themselves in danger of being discovered shows that they are selfless and caring and that both Nelly and Charley are very dear to them.

The text is written from the perspective of an omniscient narrator who follows Nelly's perspective. Hence, the reader gets an insight into her feelings. The text is, therefore, more personal and can help make the reader more empathetic towards Nelly.

The language is simple on the whole and the Laffeys seem to be using a simple version of English to ensure that Nelly understands them ("You come live here, Nelly. You come all time, eh?", l. 52). This shows affection between these three characters.

George's offer to give Nelly and her son refuge on their land in an old store shed also shows affection for the Aborigine, as this, too, was not allowed by the government.

Nelly trusts this family and knows that she is safe with them; otherwise she would not be hiding there. However, she feels unfairly treated, hurt and lost, as she is not allowed to live with her family, as an Aborigine with all her traditions, respected

and in peace. Her thoughts (ll. 28–31) show just how confused she is, how wild her emotions are: she doesn't think in grammatically correct sentences. Hence, the reader gets an insight into her emotional state.
The title of the story underlines the desperate situation Nelly is in: her heart is with her family and her home, which she is unable to return to. It is impossible for her to find another home.

Zu 3: a) Diese Aufgabe geht über den Text hinaus und setzt zusätzliche Kenntnisse voraus.
Die Schüler und Schülerinnen zeigen die Hintergründe zur *Stolen Generation* auf und gehen anschließend kritisch auf die Behandlung der Aborigines durch die Weißen anhand von Nellys Schicksal ein (z. B.: 100,000 Aboriginal children were forcibly taken between 1910 and 1970, these were known as *Stolen Generation*, this had profound consequences on the Aboriginal community, see ***Copy 18***). Sie kommen dabei zu einem Ergebnis, wie sie diese Zeit, die Taten und ihre Konsequenzen für das Leben der Aborigines bewerten.

b) Dear Jackie,

The police came looking for us again today. George and Mag were so strong and managed to keep both Charley and me hidden. The fear of being discovered, of having our son taken away by those people nearly kills me!
George asked me after the police had gone whether we would like to stay up here and move into the old store shed. He even offered you paid work so you could be with us. But can you imagine what this would mean to me? I would have to give in to this horrible situation. I would accept that these people take everything away from me, my family, you, my ancestry. They destroy our dreams and traditions. We are worth nothing!
Though I can't help asking myself whether we would be safe here. George and Mag would do anything to protect us. They would keep us from these white people and not let them take the last thing that is dear to me: our son.
Jackie, help me to decide – what am I supposed to do?
I love and miss you.

Always yours,
Nelly

Does Australia have a national identity?

Cavan Hogue
Centre for Policy Development (July 20th, 2005)

All countries create national myths and national identities which may or may not bear some resemblance to reality. In many cases, views of national identity may change or may be disputed. The nation state is a relatively recent invention and some would argue that it does more harm than good. Benedict Anderson calls nations 'imagined political communities'.

[...] While older people in particular still look nostalgically back to Mother England, many Australians question our traditional identity as tourist class British. An increasingly large percentage of the Australian population does not have a British heritage. So, if we are not British, what are we? It is easy to say that we are just Australians but what does that mean? What are the symbols and the characteristics that distinguish an Australian from someone else? It cannot be race, religion or language because we don't have our own. We don't really seem to have a clear answer to this question.

In one sense, the Aborigines are the only true Australians in that they are uniquely Australian and have been here for millennia. However, they make up 2% of our population and there is no single aboriginal language or culture. Other Australians do not share the mystical connection with their land which characterises aboriginal societies. Therefore, our aboriginal heritage does not provide a basis for the creation of a unifying national identity for all contemporary Australians.

Despite our brave rhetoric, we have never been comfortable standing independently on our own two feet and recent trends to identify us as part of 'The West' go back to seeking our identity as part of a greater whole (eg the British Empire). Our history has given us the same head of state as the UK, PNG, and a number of Caribbean countries but so long as we have a foreigner as our head of state, then we cannot use that office as a symbol of a separate national identity.

UK (*abbr.*) United Kingdom
PNG (*abbr.*) Papua New Guinea

American influence has grown rapidly over the last few decades and, thanks to TV, many Australians know more about American history than they do about their own. However, this does not seem to provide us with the basis for a national identity unless we plan on becoming the 51st state.

[...] So if we are not Aborigines, not British, not European, not Asian and not American, what are we? What myths and symbols can we use to create and maintain a national identity that unifies us and gives us a sense of being Australian? One possible answer is that we should just get on with our daily lives without worrying too much about who we think we are. This has some attraction but human beings are herd animals and most of us feel the need to belong to a group and to feel pride in that group.

We are evolving from being true Britons into a multicultural society whose people have many origins. Multiculturalism has many benefits but it can inhibit the creation of a clear national identity. Japan and Germany in the 1930s had clear national identities so this may not be a bad thing.

Our national identity, then, is a work in progress where the future is more important than the past. We should promote Australians as a people who value tolerance, equality, the peaceful solutions of disputes, and a spirit of cooperation. Of course, some of us are none of these things but national identity is all about what we think we should be rather than what some of us regrettably are. We have traditionally been laid back about our patriotism – except in sport – and this may be a good thing. We are building a new society which is not yet finished but pride in ourselves does not mean we have to dislike others. Patriotism based on dislike of other groups is a very dangerous thing as European history in the last century has taught us.

Perhaps the best we can do is to define an Australian as one who lives here, is a citizen and accepts certain core values which characterise Australian society. A defining feature of Australian identity might be that we are relaxed about it and that we reject xenophobia and jingoism? As Popeye the sailor man put it: I am what I am and that's what I am.

http://wpdev.cpd.org.au/2005/07/does-australia-have-a-national-identity/ [9.11.2010]

Cavan Hogue is a former Australian diplomat who served at ambassadorial level in Mexico, Kuala Lumpur, Moscow, Bangkok and at the United Nations in New York. He is a former Director of the National Thai Centre at the Australian National University.

Assignments

1. Describe Cavan Hogue's view on Australian nationality and explain how he answers the question of whether Australia has a national identity. (Comprehension)

2. Analyse how the author's use of language and the arguments he applies reveal Cavan Hogue's attitude towards an Australian national identity. (Analysis)

3. Choose one of the following two tasks:

a) Based on your knowledge about Australia's past and present, comment on the question of whether Australia does have a national identity and decide whether you agree with Hogue's attitude. (Comment)

or

b) Write a letter to Cavan Hogue, taking a stand on whether you agree or not with his point of view. (Creative task)

Erwartungshorizont zu Klausur 2

Zu 1: Cavan Hogue answers the question of whether Australia has a national identity by firstly stating several aspects about how Australian identity cannot be defined and that do not belong to the concept of an Australian nationality.

First of all, he refers back to Australia's British past. He emphasizes that only older people can identify with this; most Australians, however, do not have a British heritage. In his opinion, Australia does not have its own race, religion or language.

Secondly, Hogue points out that only the Aborigines can count as true Australians. However, they only make up 2% of the population and there is no one Aboriginal language or culture. Hence, the Aboriginal culture can't serve as a basis for Australian identity.

Furthermore, the lack of political independence and the fact that the British queen is still the head of state is also no basis for a national identity.

A fourth point Hogue makes is the fact that Australia has been influenced by the American culture, largely through television.

The author sums up that Australians cannot be defined as Aborigines, British, European, Asian or American. He stresses again that it is important for human beings to belong to a group and be able to be proud of it.

One conclusion Hogue draws from this is that Australia has a multicultural society, which makes it difficult to have a clear national identity.

Hence, in Hogue's view, Australian identity is a work in progress and he pleads for tolerance, equality, peace and a cooperative spirit.

His final conclusion is that an Australian could be defined as somebody who lives in Australia and accepts the values mentioned above.

Zu 2: Cavan Hogue's use of language and the arguments he applies reveal Cavan Hogue's attitude towards an Australian national identity. The author structures the text in such a way that he firstly deconstructs aspects commonly associated with Australia, but which are not helpful in the definition of an Australian identity and do not belong to the concept of an Australian nationality. Then he continues to state what Australia is or at least could be. This structure supports his ideas, since he takes arguments that could be used by his readers and explains why they are not useful in defining an Australian identity. Overall, his use of language is quite simple and straightforward which makes the text accessible for a wide range of readers, even those whose English is not very fluent.

One of the most striking features is the use of the personal pronouns "we" and "our", not only addressing readers but also including them in his argumentation. Furthermore, this shows that he includes himself in the process of defining an Australian identity.

The use of rhetorical questions also helps to make the text more communicative and involves the readers, who are invited to answer these questions for themselves.

The use of enumerations supports the reading flow. Moreover, the use of the auxiliary "may" gives the impression that he is not rigid in his views and open for discussion.

Finally, in quoting a popular cartoon character, Hogue uses humour in order to make the issue more light-hearted.

Zu 3: a) Diese Aufgabe geht über den Text hinaus und setzt zusätzliche Kenntnisse voraus.
Die Schülerinnen und Schüler listen die unterschiedlichen Aspekte einer australischen Identität auf und können sich so auf Aspekte, die sie in dieser Unterrichtsreihe gelernt haben, beziehen. Dabei können sie auf die Nutzung Australiens als Strafgefangenenkolonie in der Vergangenheit eingehen sowie auf die Prägung durch die Rinderzucht und die in der Bevölkerung weit verbreitete Tätigkeit als Viehtreiber und Farmer im Outback. Auch die Diskriminierung der Aborigines durch die Weißen sollte Erwähnung finden sowie die Tatsache, dass sehr viele Australier sowohl britische als auch indigene Vorfahren haben.
Sie kommen dabei zu einem Ergebnis, wie sie die Frage nach der australischen Nationalität für sich selbst beantworten und Hogues Argumente bewerten.

b) Dear Mr Cavan Hogue,

I'm writing in response to your article "Does Australia have a national identity?" which I found very interesting and would like to comment on.
It is interesting that after all these centuries, Australia is still under British influence and I believe that it is indeed obstructive to the process of creating a national identity if a foreigner is the head of the Australian state. However, I do not see the American influence as a necessarily bad thing, as we are also very much influenced by the American culture in Germany, which only adds a certain cultural variety.
On the one hand, I do agree with your point of view that the Australian identity is indeed a work in progress. It does remind me of the so-called melting pot idea in the USA. Australia is very multicultural and it is essential to be tolerant towards each other and guarantee equality between the different cultures. Overall, I share your point of view that being in a group and taking pride in it gives a great sense of belonging and that this shouldn't be based on dislike of other groups. I like the fact that Australians are laid back about their patriotism.
On the other hand, I do not agree with your point of view that the best way to define an Australian is one who lives there as this is put in too simple terms. It would need to be defined for which length of time somebody has to have lived in Australia to count as an Australian, whether he or she has to be fluent in English and whether he or she views him or herself as Australian. In this respect, it would be interesting to read about any further ideas you might have.

Yours sincerely

Component 1

Convicts – Contributing to Australia's national identity?

1.1 Getting started – Speaking about Australian identity

Zur Einführung in die koloniale Vergangenheit Australiens sollen die Schülerinnen und Schüler sich mit der Bedeutung der *convicts* für die australische Identität auseinandersetzen. Nach Schätzungen von Experten dürften bis zu 4 Millionen Australier Nachfahren der seit 1789 aus Großbritannien und Irland deportierten *convicts* sein.
Die Zitate, die zu Stundenbeginn mithilfe von ***Copy 1*** dargeboten werden, dokumentieren die stereotype Vorstellung von Australien als einem Land, das durch die hohe Zahl von Siedlern mit krimineller Vergangenheit geprägt wurde und dessen nationaler Charakter bis heute weitgehend von der Mentalität der *convicts* geprägt wurde.
Gegen dieses Bild stehen jedoch statistische Zahlen, die einen nur geringen Einfluss auf das nationale Selbstverständnis der Australier dokumentieren. Die im Rahmen des *Australian Constitutional Referendum Survey* (1999) erhobenen Daten (vgl. Tranter/Donoghue 2003) zeigen, dass trotz des hohen Anteils von *convicts* an der Gesamtzahl britischer Siedler im 18. und 19. Jahrhundert heute nur ein geringer Teil der Australier mit Stolz über die *convict past* berichten, während nahezu zwei Drittel der Bewohner keine direkte familiäre Verbindung zu diesen frühen Siedlern sehen und diese für das nationale Selbstverständnis als nicht relevant ansehen.
Interessanterweise variieren diese Zahlen aber sowohl bezüglich regionaler Aspekte (in Tasmanien, dem früheren Van-Diemens-Land, glaubt jeder zweite Befragte an eine familiäre Verbindung zu den *convicts*) als auch mit Blick auf Geschlecht, sozialem Status und Alter: Während die ältere Bevölkerung Australiens und Australier mit hohen Bildungsabschlüssen die Bedeutung der *convicts* für die australische Identität gerne negieren, sehen vor allem jüngere Australier, Frauen und einfache Arbeiter in den *convicts* durchaus ein wichtiges Element für die Entwicklung australischer Identität. In den letzten Jahren haben daher entsprechende Angebote zur Recherche der eigenen Familiengeschichte in Australien an Bedeutung gewonnen und viele Australier berichten mit Stolz über ihre ganz persönlichen Bezüge zur *convict past* (vgl. Angebote zur Internetrecherche wie z. B. http://www.slq.qld.gov.au/info/fh/convicts).
Diese Ergebnisse sollen von den Schülerinnen und Schülern diskutiert und problematisiert werden, um die Relevanz der ersten *short story* für das Reihenthema erkennen zu lassen und um sie angemessen einordnen zu können.

Convicts – Shaping Australia's identity?

STEP 1:
The following quotes refer to Australia's convict past. What sort of image or stereotype about the Australians do they reflect?

All our best heroes are losers.
Richard Glover

A few years ago we colonised this place with some of our finest felons, thieves, muggers, alcoholics and prostitutes, a strain of depravity which I believe has contributed greatly to this country's amazing vigour and enterprise.
Ian Wooldridge

Depravity moral corruption, wickedness

The extraordinary rapid growth which has followed upon settlement of the scum of the earth on the shores of Australia would make it appear that in colonisation it is as in gardening, the more your foundations consist of dung, the more rapid and striking the production.
David Monroe

They are not a nation of snobs like the English or of extravagant boasters like the Americans or of reckless profligates like the French, they are simply a nation of drunkards.
Marcus Clark

STEP 2:
When asked about whether they are (or might be) descendants from one of the convicts who were sent to Australia during the first period of British settlement, people in Australia gave the following answers:

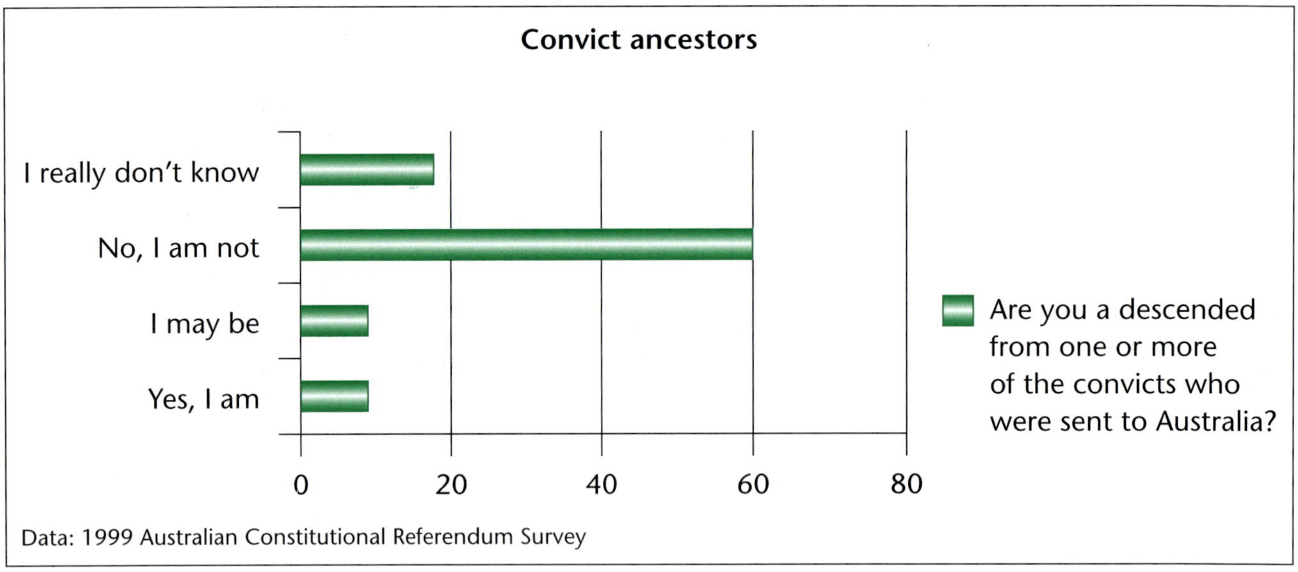

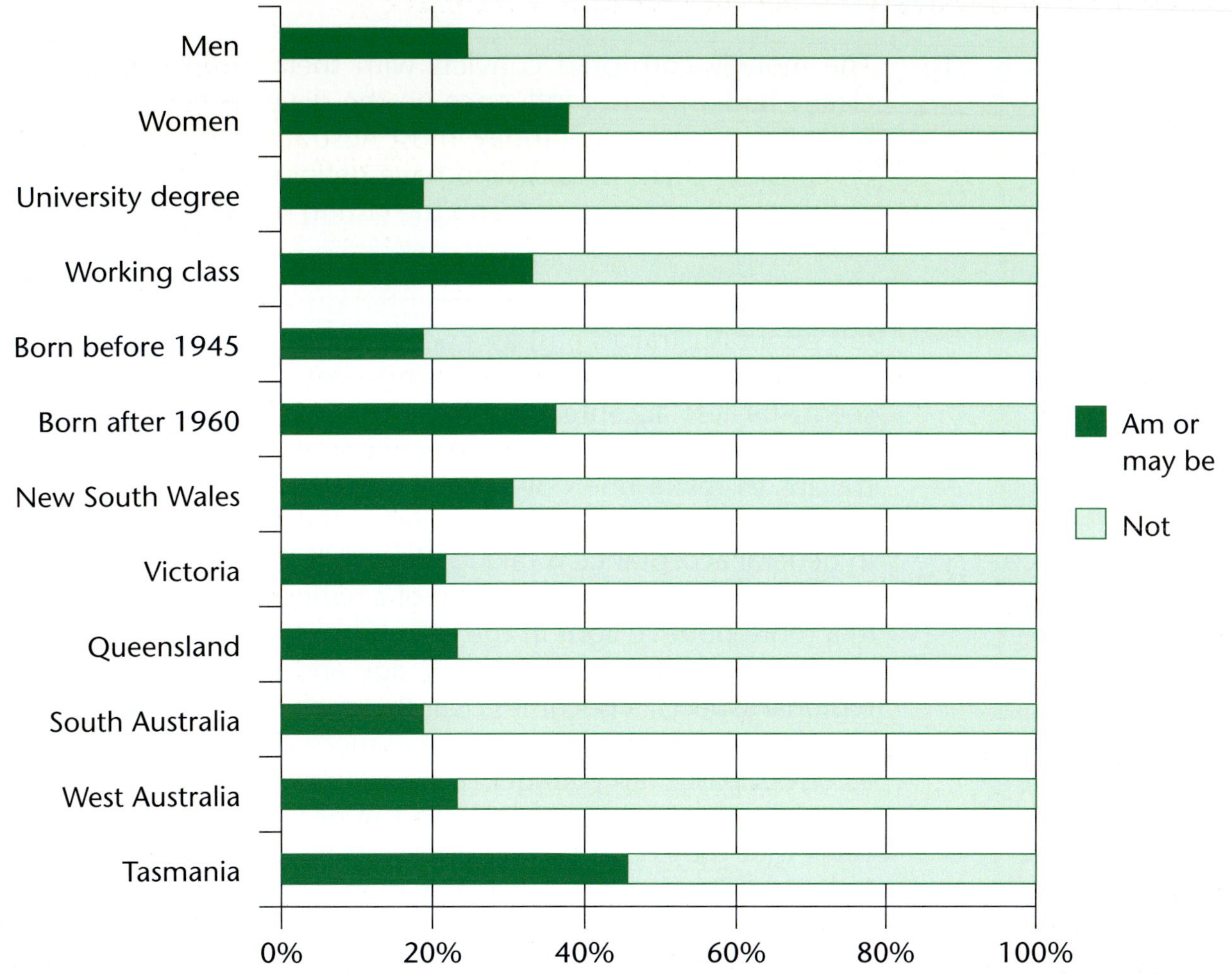

Data: 1999 Australian Constitutional Referendum Survey

Assignments

1. Does convict ancestry have a positive or negative influence on Australian identity?
2. Why do you think most Australians neglect their (possible) convict history?
3. What role do age, sex, social status and regional aspects play?

Lösungsvorschlag zu *Copy 1:*

1. The morally corrupted convicts with their criminal background clearly had a positive influence on the development of a distinct Australian identity. Still today, most Australians, like Richard Glover, consider them heroes who have definitely contributed to the rapid growth of the nation and the lasting success of the colonization.

2./3. While it seems to be widely accepted on a more general level to talk about Australia's past as a penal colony and the positive influence of the convicts on the development of a national identity, it seems far less accepted to have convict ancestors in one's own family. However, it has become very popular among younger Australians to relate one's own family history to the convict past of Australia. Therefore, one can assume that that a gradual change in general acceptance is taking place and that the contribution of the convicts to the development of a national identity will be seen in a more positive light in the near future.
Especially when focusing on sex, age and social status as well as regional aspects, it becomes clear that men of middle age and with a higher social status seem to have more difficulties in accepting a convict past than younger (especially female) Australians with a working class background. While the percentage of people who think that they have convict ancestors is quite low in South Australia and Victoria, it is reasonably higher in Tasmania (former Van Diemen's Land). Large numbers of convicts have clearly influenced the history of Tasmania and have contributed to national identity – far more than in Victoria and other states where the number of convicts was much smaller.

1.2 Exploring the convict past

Nachdem die Schülerinnen und Schüler sich in der ersten Stunde bereits mit der Relevanz der *convicts* für das australische Selbstbewusstsein kritisch auseinandergesetzt haben, sollen in der folgenden (Doppel-)Stunde die *convicts* und deren spezifische Lebensumstände näher in den Blick genommen werden.
Die Schüler erarbeiten dazu in arbeitsteiliger Gruppenarbeit wesentliche Aspekte zur Geschichte der *convicts* in Australien. Die Ergebnisse werden mit den anderen Mitschülern ausgetauscht und diskutiert.
Hierzu eignet sich die Präsentationsmethode „*One stay, three stray*". Nach der Erarbeitung der drei Arbeitsblätter ***(Copies 2–4)*** in Gruppen bleibt ein Gruppenmitglied am Tisch zurück und informiert die Schülergruppen, die an den Tisch kommen, während die übrigen drei Gruppenmitglieder in die anderen Gruppen gehen, um sich über die dortigen Arbeitsergebnisse zu informieren. (Eine ausführliche Darstellung der Methode mit Kopiervorlagen und *language support* findet sich bei Grieser-Kindel/Henseler/Möller 2009, S. 111.)
Bei Bedarf kann die Auseinandersetzung mit der Thematik auch ausgeweitet werden und z. B. durch fächerverbindende Aktivitäten oder durch gemeinsame bilinguale Module ergänzt werden.

Australian convict songs

In your group, analyse the following two Australian convict songs. What do they tell you about the convicts, their alleged crimes and their living conditions in the penal colony?

a) Botany Bay

Farewell to Old England forever,
Farewell to my old pals as well,
Farewell to the well known Old Bailee,
Where I once used to be such a swell,
Where I once used to be such a swell.

Singing too-rall, li-oo-rall, li-ad-di-ty,
Singing too-rall, li-oo-rall, li-ay,
Singing too-rall, li-oo-rall, li-ad-di-ty
Oh we are bound for Botany Bay
Oh we are bound for Botany Bay.

There's the captain as is our commandeer,
There's bosun and all the ship's crew,
There's first and the second class passengers,
Knows what we poor convicts goes through,
Knows what we poor convicts goes through.

Chorus

'Taint leaving Old England we cares about,
'Taint 'cos we mispells wot we knows,
But becos all we light finger'd gentry,
Hop's around with a log on our toes,
Hop's around with a log on our toes.

Chorus

Oh had I the wings of a turtle-dove,
I'd soar on my pinions so high,
Slap bang to the arms of my Polly love,
And in her sweet presence I'd die,
And in her sweet presence I'd die.

Chorus

Now all my young Dookies and Duchesses,
Take warning from what I've to say,
Mind all is your own as you touch-es-es,
Or you'll find us in Botany Bay,
Or you'll find us in Botany Bay.

Text and music: Florian Pascal

Old Bailee Central Criminal Court in London
swell (*coll.*) important person

bosun a ship's officer in charge of equipment and the crew

b) Jim Jones

Oh, listen for a moment, lads,
and hear me tell my tale;
How, o'er the sea from England's shore,
I was compelled to sail.
The jury says, 'He's guilty, sir!'
and says the judge, says he –
'For life, Jim Jones, I'm sending you
across the stormy sea.

'And take my tip before you ship
to join the iron gang,
Don't be too gay[1] at Botany Bay,
or else you'll surely hang.
Or else you'll hang, he says,
says he, 'and after that, Jim Jones,
high upon the gallows tree
the crows will pick your bones.

'You'll have no chance for mischief then –
remember what I say:
They'll flog the mischief out of you
when you get to Botany Bay!'
The waves were high upon the sea,
the wind blew up in gales;
I'd rather be drowned in misery
than go to New South Wales.

For night and day the irons clang,
and, like poor galley slaves,
We toil and moil and when we die
must fill dishonoured graves.
But by and by I'll break my chains;
into the bush I'll go;
And join the bold bushrangers there –
Jack Donahoe and Co.

And some dark night when everything
is silent in this town
I'll shoot the tyrants one and all
and shoot the floggers down.
I'll give the law a little shock,
remember what I say,
They'll yet regret they sent Jim Jones
in chains to Botany Bay.

Text and music: traditional Australian song, composer unknown

[1] **gay** happy

The convict system

In your group, read the following background information about the convict system. What does the text reveal about the living conditions of convicts in the penal colony?

Between 1788 and 1868, more than 165,000 convicts were transported to Australia. The first 751 convicts arrived with the First Fleet at Botany Bay on January 18, 1788. Two additional fleets with convicts arrived in 1790 and 1791, long before the first free settlers arrived in Australia in 1793.
Governor Phillip (1788–1792) founded a system of labour in which the convicts were employed on public works and helped to establish a permanent settlement around the Sydney cove. Thousands of prisoners worked as brick makers, carpenters, shepherds and farmers and helped to build roads and public buildings or worked for the free settlers on their farms. Female convicts, which amounted to up to twenty percent of the first convicts, were employed as domestic servants to the officers or were sent to hospitals and the rapidly growing textile factories. The convicts were generally considered as cheap labour to advance and develop the British colony in Australia.
For a long time, convicts formed the majority of the colony's population and a growing number of freed convicts were granted land and became free settlers themselves. Additionally, many freed convicts were appointed to public positions and further helped to develop the country.

Convict lives

During the first years of the penal colony, the convicts usually wore their ordinary civilian clothing. However, with the rapidly growing number of free settlers, it became necessary to clearly distinguish the convicts from the other settlers. Therefore, a sort of uniform was created which should be worn by the convicts. Their food very much depended on what was available in the colony. As it was very difficult to cultivate crops, supplies from England were very much relied on for food in the beginning. The weekly supply of food for a government employed convict included the following rations.
The food rations of the average convict, however, were usually higher than the average diet of a free worker in Industrial Great Britain (the average diet of an industrial worker in the early 19th century in Britain and Ireland reached up to 2600 calories) and also higher than the diets of prisoners in the Nazi labour camps in the 1940s.

New South Wales Penal Colony (1789)		Auschwitz labour camp (1944)	
Beef	3 kg	Beef	0.080 kg
Bread	3 kg	Bread	2.4 kg
Maize meal (porridge)	1.3 kg	Vegetable soup	3.5 l
Sugar	0.5 kg	–	
Tea		("Ersatz")coffee	
3100 calories per day		1700–2000 calories per day *(official rations according to NS administration – in reality, most prisoners received much less, if anything at all)*	

In one of his letters home, a convict wrote to his parents:

"As to my living I find it better than ever I expected thank God. I want for nothing in that respect. As for tea and sugar, I almost could swim in it. I am allowed 2 pounds of sugar and ¼ pound of tea per week and plenty of tobacco and good white bread and sometimes beef sometimes mutton sometimes pork this I have every day. Plenty of fruit puddings in the season of all sorts. And I have two suits of cloths a year and three pairs of shoes in a year and I want for nothing but my liberty."[1]

While the nutrition might be considered appropriate in contrast to the diet of the average British worker, one should not forget the hard working conditions with more than 12 hours of hard physical work under fairly adverse climatic conditions (extremely high and low temperatures, strong wind chill, rain), which could lead to malnutrition and diseases (especially among so called 'convict gangs'). Finally, regular punishment (like flogging and leg irons) also contributed to the prisoners' health status.
In order to maintain discipline and order, convicts could be flogged (with the so called 'cat-o-nine tails') for the smallest of offences, like swearing, being drunk, stealing and other minor crimes. Convicts who ran way from their work were often sentenced to work in leg irons for at least 6 months and up to 3 years.
On the other hand, well-behaved convicts could be rewarded by being given responsible jobs, allowed time away from the barracks or finally even be given a ticket-of-leave. This meant the convict was allowed to work for money and own land but was not allowed to leave the area (or even return back home to England), which was only allowed after a conditional pardon (which allowed him to live anywhere in the colony) or an absolute pardon (which allowed him to go anywhere).
After the convict had served his or her sentence, they received a certificate of freedom.

[1] Richard Dillinham, letter from Van Diemen's Land to his parents, dated 29 September 1836. Published in "The Mail", Newsletter of Descendants of Convicts Group, Melbourne, May/June 1999.

Convicts and their crimes

In your group, read the following background information about the convict past of Australia. What do you learn about the convicts and the reasons they were sent to Australia. What does the convict past of Australia imply for the development of a national identity?

Text 1: **Online records highlight Australia's convict past**

More than 2 million Britons and an estimated 4 million Australians are related to convicts deported from Britain to Australia in the 18th and 19th centuries, genealogists say.

The figures come as online family history sites www.ancestry.co.uk and www.ancestry.com.au launched what they said was the most comprehensive online collection of convict transit records from the 80-year period the policy ran.

Based on the records, demographics, birth rates, census data and migration and emigration patterns, the sites estimated 22 per cent of living Australians had a convict ancestor while there was a one in 30 chance for Britons.

Information that can now be accessed includes the names, dates and place of conviction, terms of sentence, names of ships, departure dates and colonies where most of the 163,021 people were sent.

Details were taken from the British authorities' Convict Transportation Registers 1788–1868 and three other documents from Australia itself detailing the names of convicts and settlers.

A spokesman for both sites, Josh Hanna, said in a statement that Australia's convict history was well-documented, with even Prime Minister John Howard claiming less than law-abiding ancestors.

But he added: "This is the first time that these unique records have ever been brought together in one place online, making them accessible to so many."

Convict deportation peaked in 1833 when 36 ships transported nearly 7,000 people to Britain's former colony. The journey lasted eight months, six of which were spent at sea and two in ports for resupply and repairs to vessels.

The records show that 83 per cent of convicts were male aged 15 to 30 and 75 per cent were unskilled workers.

Seventy per cent were English; 24 percent were Irish; and 5 per cent Scottish. The oldest was about 60 and the youngest nine.

But although 2 per cent were guilty of serious crimes such as murder or assault, the vast majority – 87 per cent of men and 91 per cent of women – were convicted of minor offences, particularly property crimes.

They included stealing fish from a river or pond, embezzlement, receiving or buying stolen goods, setting fire to underwood or petty theft.

Notable convicts include Irishman Red Kelly, who was found guilty of stealing two pigs and sent to Tasmania. He moved to the state of Victoria after his release, married and had a son, Ned Kelly, the famous outlaw.

Also among them were Elizabeth Thackery, the first female convict to set foot in Australia after being found guilty of stealing five handkerchiefs, and West Indian John Caesar, the first black convict.

http://www.abc.net.au/news/stories/2007/07/25/1987575.htm [09.12.10]

Text 2: **Convict crimes**

Piracy: In 1827, a small ship manned by nine Greek sailors robbed a British ship bound for Malta. The Greeks were later caught, and brought to trial. In their defence, the Greeks argued that, under international law, they had been entitled to intercept and rob a vessel destined for a port occupied by Turkey; their enemy. Initially, the men were sentenced to death, but concern about the validity of the English laws led to seven of the men being sent to Australia instead.

Irish rebels: In 1690, Catholic Ireland was conquered by Protestant England. The English subsequently passed laws that Catholics could not vote, could not enter university, could not be members of Parliament, could not own a gun, could not travel more than 5 miles from home and could not teach in Protestant schools. Three-quarters of Irish land was owned by English Protestants who rented it to the Irish farmers. If rent was not paid, bailiffs would take anything moveable such as livestock or furniture and then evict the family. To survive, many Irish were forced to a life to crime. Other Irish struggled to realize political change. In March 1798 Ireland was declared to be in a state of insurrection. Under the Insurrection Act, Magistrates and Military Officers were empowered to arrest and punish, by death or otherwise, according to their discretion, people committing treasonable acts or even suspected of treason. An Indemnity Act protected them from suits for illegal acts committed by them in suppressing a rebellion, so that many thousands were flogged, tortured, transported or executed without any judicial trial or investigation.

Naval mutineers: Life was difficult for sailors in the 18th century. They could be flogged without reason, food was scarce and pay almost non-existent. It had been said that 'being a sailor in a ship is being in gaol with the chance of being drowned. 'Mutinies were usually dealt with by hangings. Occasionally; however, the mutineers were sent to Australia.

Black South Africans: From 1828 to 1834, South Africa deported many blacks that were not political prisoners, but had transgressed white South African laws.

Pickpockets: Often the pickpockets were well organized gangs that targeted social gatherings of the rich and famous. In a crowd, the pickpocket's victim would not feel a hand relieving them of their valuables. As soon as the item was stolen, it would be passed to an assistant (often an elegantly dressed lady) who would hurry to another part of town.

Orphans: Convicts as young as 10 were transported to Australia. Such children had no parents, no homes and no schools hence took to a life of crime to survive.

Women: The Convict women were usually reported to have been low-class women, foul mouthed and with loose morals; however, this was not always the case. Often women would commit crimes deliberately to be able to join their husbands in the colony. Punishments for women included an iron collar fastened round the neck or having her head shaved as a mark of disgrace. Often these punishments were for moral misdemeanours, such as being 'found in the yard of an inn in an indecent posture for an immoral purpose'. Women would often intentionally offend the authorities by bearing their back side or name the priest when asked who the father of their child was.

Servants: In a house of nobility, if an item went missing or was misplaced, the servant was usually blamed. Convictions were assured even when there was a lack of evidence. Other servants formed relationships with their masters and were accused of theft when the master wanted the relationship to end.

Aborigines: Aborigines became Convicts for either defending their home or cultural misunderstandings. Warriors such as Yagan, Pelmulwuy and Musquito were outlawed for enforcing Aboriginal law. Yagan and Pelmulwuy were eventually beheaded whilst Musquito was transported to Tasmania where he again made trouble and was then executed.
Other Aborigines came before the law due to cultural misunderstandings. In nomadic societies, there was no concept of individual possession rather what is owned by friends is owned by all. Consequently, the Aborigines frequently walked off with any European item that held their interest. Subsequently, many officials found it ironic that they had established a penal colony amongst the greatest thieves on earth.

Official crimes list: The following is the list of crimes that was punishable by transportation

1.) All theft above the value of one shilling.
2.) Thefts under the value of one shilling.
3.) Receiving stolen goods, jewels and plate.
4.) Stealing lead, iron or copper.
5.) Stealing ore from black lead mines.
6.) Stealing from furnished lodgings.
7.) Setting fire to underwood.
8.) Stealing letters.
9.) Assault with intent to rob.
10.) Stealing fish from a pond or river.
11.) Stealing roots, trees or plants.
12.) Bigamy.
13.) Assaulting, cutting or burning clothes.

http://www.convictcreations.com/history/crimes.htm [09.12.10] (adapted)

John Morgan: The life and adventures of William Buckley

In your group, read the following information about Australia's most famous convict, William Buckley. What does the text reveal about the convicts, the reasons for being sent to Australia and the living conditions of convicts in the penal colony? Why did the convict William Buckley contribute to the development of an Australian identity?

"I was born in the year 1780 at Macclesfield, in the County of Cheshire, England. My parents were humble people, who honestly provided for the support of themselves, and a family of two girls and two boys, by cultivating a small farm in the neighbourhood. What has become of my brothers and sisters, is not known to me ..."

As a young man, Buckley became an apprentice bricklayer:
"I remember, that from some circumstance or other, I was adopted by my mother's father, and that I was sent by him to an evening school, where I was taught to read; and that when about fifteen years of age, I was apprenticed by the same good old man to a Mr. Robert Wyatt, a Bricklayer, residing in that neighbourhood, to be taught the art and mystery of building houses for other people to live in – it being my fate, as will presently be seen, during thirty-two years, to inhabit dwellings of a very different description, having for their roofs only the wide spread of heaven.
Having been removed in the first instance from the immediate charge of my parents, I was, I suppose, not so strictly treated by the old people as I should have been, as a boy, and hence the restraints imposed on me by my master, and his very proper endeavours to make me useful and industrious, were considered hardships and punishments, unnecessarily and improperly inflicted. This feeling, in time, completely unsettled me, and my uncontrolled discontent mastering my boyish reason, when I was about nineteen, I determined to enlist as a soldier, and to win glorious laurels in thc battlefield."

WILLIAM BUCKLEY,
THE WILD WHITE MAN.

As a soldier in the King's Foot Regiment, he went to Holland in 1799 to fight against Napoleon, under the command of the Duke of York. After returning to London, he was convicted of stealing cloth; which he maintained he was carrying for a woman and didn't know was stolen. He was subsequently sentenced to transportation to New South Wales for 14 years:

"One day, crossing the Barrack Yard where our regiment was quartered, a woman whom I did not know requested me to carry a piece of cloth to a woman of the Garrison to be made up [into clothing]. I was stopped with it in my possession, the property had been stolen. I was considered a thief and though innocent sentenced to transportation."

Buckley left England in April *1803*, aboard the *H.M.S. Calcutta*; They arrived in October *1803*, and anchored off the south-eastern side of the bay, near modern day *Portsea*:
"The particular locality had been chosen as the site of a penal station, it being six hundred miles from the nearest settlement, Sydney, and the chances of escape offered to the prisoner being, therefore, very few. In a short time the Marines and convicts landed, and encamped [...] A magazine and a store-house were the first public buildings commended, and the former I had been employed about three months, when I determined on endeavouring to make my escape, and to get, if possible, to Sydney. The attempt was little short of madness, for there was before me the chances of being retaken, and probable death, or other dreadful punishment; or again starvation in an unknown country inhabited by savages, with whose language and habits, I was totally unacquainted."

On December, 27th 1803, William Buckley flees from the penal colony and hides himself in the Australian bush:

"I remember a fancy coming over me, that I could have remained at that spot all the rest of my life; but this solitary desire was but temporary, for, as it was never intended that man should live alone, so are implanted in his nature, social feelings, and thoughts instinctively leading to the comforts of home, be it ever so homely, and yearnings for society, be it ever so humble."

In this moment of great loneliness, Buckley makes acquaintance with the local aboriginal tribe of the Watourong. They treat him well, teaching him how to fish, collect local food and even help him understand their language. For the next thirty-two years, he continues to live among the Watourong tribe on the Bellarine Peninsula.

On July 6th, 1835 Buckley, now wearing kangaroo skins and carrying Aboriginal weapons, finally decides to return to white society. The former convict is pardoned by Lieutenant-Governor Arthur and is given the position of an Interpreter to the natives.

Samuel Calvert: Buckley discovering himself to the early settlers (1869)

His knowledge of the Aboriginal language and culture along with his profound knowledge of the territory was of good use to the British settlers.

William Buckley died in 1856 at the age of 75, following a cart accident near Hobart.

John Morgan: The Life and Adventures of William Buckley: Thirty-Two Years a Wanderer. Hobart, MacDougall, 1852

Lösungsvorschläge:

1. Living conditions in the penal colony *(**Copies** 2 and 3)*

- Transport by ship was long and convicts had to endure bad weather conditions, storms and were sometimes attacked by pirates.
- The living conditions in the penal colony were rather bad as well, including hard physical work under difficult climatic conditions with extremely high and low temperatures, strong winds and heavy rain and reduced food provisions, which sometimes led to malnutrition and diseases among convicts.
- Convicts got punished for the slightest offences (e.g. being drunk, swearing).
- Well-behaved convicts could be rewarded by getting a ticket-of-leave or a conditional pardon, sometimes even leading to a certificate of freedom.

2. Reasons for being sent to Australia *(**Copy** 4)*

- Most convicts sent to Australia had committed only minor offenses, mostly property crimes like theft, poaching, receiving or buying stolen goods, setting fire to underwood etc.
- Only two percent of the convicts were guilty of serious crimes such as murder or assault.

3. Consequence for the development of a distinct Australian identity *(**Copy** 5)*

- Probably more than 4 million Australians have convict ancestors.
- Currently there is a growing interest in family history among Australians; researching details of one's own convict past has become quite popular.
- Relating oneself to one of the 165.000 convicts being sent to Australia makes oneself a 'true Australian'.
- Famous convicts like William Buckley have served as a role model for Australian identity. Their strong will and determination, questioning of authority and their adaptability to the new living conditions made them respected members of Australian society and have helped to shape Australian identity.

1.3 Understanding convict life

In dieser Stunde soll durch Bezug auf den Auszug aus Marcus Clarkes Roman *For the term of his natural life* ein vertieftes Verständnis für die Haftbedingungen in den Strafkolonien erreicht werden. In Clarkes Roman ist der Protagonist zu Unrecht verhaftet und nach Australien deportiert worden, was den Perspektivwechsel und die Identifikation der Schülerinnen und Schüler mit dem Protagonisten Rufus Dawes und seiner Leidenssituation noch einmal erleichtert. Zugleich wird deutlich, dass die britischen Aufseher nicht regelkonformes Verhalten sofort und mit aller Brutalität bestrafen. Als vorrangiges Ziel im Umgang mit den Häftlingen gilt es nach Aussage des Lagerkommandanten Frere, den Willen der Häftlinge zu brechen. Vor diesem Hintergrund erscheint die Geschichte des Gefangenen Glancy und das Verhalten des *muster-master* Stoneman ebenfalls in einem anderen Licht.

Flogging a convict at Noreton Bay (1836, artist unknown)

Die Stunde wird mit einem Bild eingeleitet, auf der das *flogging*, das Auspeitschen von Häftlingen mit der *cat-o'-nine-tails*, der neunschwänzigen Katze (einer Riemenpeitsche mit insgesamt neun geflochtenen Tauenden), gezeigt wird.

Die Schüler sollen die Lebensumstände der *convicts* in Australien, basierend auf den Informationen der vorangegangenen Stunde (vgl. ***Copies 2–5***), beschreiben und problematisieren. Im Anschluss soll der Romanauszug von den Schülerinnen und Schülern gelesen werden, wobei die inhaltliche Auseinandersetzung mit den Haftumständen in der *penal colony* und der Abgleich mit dem Vorwissen der Schülerinnen und Schüler im Vordergrund stehen sollte.

Marcus Clarke: For the term of his natural life

The following excerpt is taken from Marcus Clarke's novel *For the term of his natural life* (1870). It deals with the story of Rufus, a young man who is being sent to the prison colony of Van Diemen's Land (today's Tasmania) for a crime he did not commit.
In the penal colony, Dawes experiences regular punishment and violence by the wardens. One day, Mr Troke, one of the wardens, sets a trap in order to find concealed tobacco with the convicts and during night, while Dawes is fully asleep, imitates the voice of another convict and asks for some tobacco:

Rufus Dawes was but half awake, and on repeating his request, Troke felt something put into his hand. He grasped Dawes' arm and struck a light. He had got his man this time. Dawes had conveyed to his (fancied) friend a piece of tobacco almost as big as the top joint of his little finger.
One can understand the feelings of a man entrapped by such base means. Rufus Dawes no sooner saw the hated face of Warder Troke peering over his hammock, than he sprang out, and exerting to the outmost his powerful muscles, slung out his left hand from his hip with such tremendous violence that Mr Troke was knocked fairly off his legs into the arms of the incoming constables. A desperate struggle took place, at the end of which, the convict, overpowered by numbers, was borne senseless to the cells, gagged, and chained to the ring-bolt on the bare flags. While in this condition, he was dreadfully beaten by five or six constables.
To this maimed and manacled rebel was the Commandant ushered by Troke the next morning.
'Ha! ha! My man,' says the Commandant. 'Here you are again, you see. How do you like this sort of thing?'
Dawes glaring, makes no answer.
'You shall have fifty lashes, my man' says Frere. 'We'll see how you'll feel then!
The fifty were duly administered, and the Commandant called the next day. The rebel was still mute.
'Give him fifty more, Mr Troke. We'll see what he's made of'.
Fifty more lashes were inflicted in the course of the morning, but still the sullen convict refused to speak. He was then treated to fourteen days' solitary confinement in one of the new cells. On being brought out and confronted with his tormentor, he merely laughed. For this he was sent back for another fourteen days; and still remaining obdurate, was flogged again, and got fourteen days more. Had the chaplain then visited him, he would have found him open to consolation, but the chaplain – so it was stated – was sick. When brought out at the conclusion of his third confinement, he was found to be in so exhausted a condition, that the doctor ordered him to the hospital. As soon as he was sufficiently recovered, Frere visited him, and finding his 'spirit' not yet 'broken', ordered that he should be put to grind maize. Dawes declined the work. So they chained his hand to one arm of the grindstone, and placed another prisoner at the other arm. As the second prisoner turned, the hand of Dawes of course revolved.
'You're not such a pebble as folks seem to think,' grinned Frere, pointing to the turning wheel.

hammock a bed made of canvas or rope mesh suspended from two supports by cords at both ends

flag (flagstone) a smooth flat piece of stone used for floors, paths etc.
maim to wound or injure someone very seriously
manacles one of two metal bands joined by a chain, for fastening a person's hands or ankles; to manacle: confine (a person or part of the body) with manacles

obdurate stubbornly refusing to change one's opinion or course of action

Upon which the indomitable poor evil straightened his sorely-tried muscles, and prevented the wheel from turning at all.

Frere gave him fifty more lashes, and sent him the next day to grind cayenne pepper. This was a punishment more dreaded by the convicts than any other. The pungent dust filled their eyes and lungs, causing them the most excruciating torments. For a man with a raw back the work was one continued agony. In four days, Rufus Dawes, emaciated, blistered, blinded, broke down.

'For God's sake, Captain Frere, kill me at once!' he said.

'No fear,' said the other, rejoiced at this proof of his power. 'You've given in; that's all I wanted. Troke, take him to the hospital.'

Marcus Clarke, *For the Term of his Natural Life*. Camberwell, VIC: Penguin 2009

indomitable impossible to subdue or defeat

pungent having a sharply strong taste or smell
excruciating intensely painful
emaciated abnormally thin or weak, especially because of illness or a lack of food

Assignments

1. What is the total number of lashes, solitary confinement and other forms of punishment Dawes experiences as a consequence of illegally keeping tobacco?
2. What is Rufus Dawes' reaction to these punishments? How would you describe his character?
3. What is revealed about the warden, Mr Troke and Captain Frere. What is their motivation or reason for Dawes' continued torture?

Lösungsvorschläge zu *Copy 6*:

1. What is the total number of lashes, solitary confinement and other forms of punishment Dawes experiences as a consequence of illegally keeping tobacco?

Dawes record of torture

Convict Dawes is …

a) severely beaten by five or six constables
b) flogged (receiving 50 lashes)
c) flogged a second time (receiving additional 50 lashes)
d) treated to fourteen days of solitary confinement
e) sentenced to additional fourteen days of solitary confinement
f) flogged (probably additional 50 lashes)
g) sentenced to another fourteen days of solitary confinement
h) ordered to grind maize and after refusing, chained to the grindstone (which painfully hurts his hands)
i) flogged again (50 more lashes)
j) ordered to grind cayenne pepper for four days

In total, Convict Dawes received the following forms of punishment as a consequence of illegally keeping tobacco:
200 lashes
42 days in solitary confinement
4 days of hard work grinding cayenne pepper
→ Severely injured, blinded, exhausted and broken down, he desperately begs to be killed at once.

2. What is Rufus Dawes' reaction to these punishments? How would you describe his character?

Despite the harsh forms of punishment and torture, Dawes remains determined not to give in and let his will be broken. He withstands the commandant's and Mr Troke's attempts to break his will by punishing him for something he did not commit. Dawes seems to be self-confident, persistent and declines to accept the injustice of the penal system.

3. What is revealed about the warden, Mr Troke and Captain Frere? What is their motivation or reason for Dawes' continued torture?

The total number of lashes and other forms of punishment indicate that the punishment is not enacted in order to maintain law and order in the penal colony, but to make an example of Convict Dawes. He is expected to submit himself to the convict system, as represented by Captain Frere and warden Troke. Dawes' unwillingness to give in leads to the escalation of violence against him.

1.4 Analysing short stories

Nachdem die Schülerinnen und Schüler sich intensiver mit dem historischen Kontext und den Lebensumständen der *convicts* auseinandergesetzt haben, kann im Folgenden die Kurzgeschichte näher betrachtet werden. Der Schwerpunkt der Auseinandersetzung mit der ersten *short story* soll dabei die vertiefte Textanalyse bilden, durch die ein Grundlagenwissen zum Gattungsbereich *short stories* sowie ein vertieftes Textsortenbewusstsein entwickelt werden soll. Da die Kurzgeschichte recht umfangreich und sprachlich sehr anspruchsvoll ist, wird eine vorbereitende häusliche Lektüre empfohlen.

In der folgenden Stunde werden die Merkmale der *short story* anhand der Definition von Werlich (1999, zitiert nach Thaler 2009: 59) mit den Schülerinnen und Schülern in Partnerarbeit erarbeitet. Dazu füllen sie nach dem Leseprozess das folgende Arbeitsblatt ***(Copy 7)*** aus. Zur sprachlichen Unterstützung sind dem Arbeitsblatt einige *useful phrases* beigefügt, die bei Bedarf (und entsprechend leistungsstarken Lerngruppen) aber auch weggelassen werden können. Zur Vertiefung oder als Element der Binnendifferenzierung kann darüber hinaus die klassische Definition von E. A. Poe genutzt werden (Anhang der Textausgabe, S. 127f.).
Für Lerngruppen, die mit den *literary devices* nicht näher vertraut sind, empfielt sich eine kurze Wiederholung der wichtigsten literarischen Stilmittel, da diese in den folgenden Kurzgeschichten immer wieder relevant sein werden.

Lösungsvorschlag zu *Copy 7*:

Characteristic features of a short story	Examples from the text
Incident	The short story portrays the escape of a convict in a penal colony in Australia. The escape, however, is not successful because convict Glancy finally returns back to the penal station of his free will.
Plot	Surprising turning point: Glancy returns to the penal station.
Characters	Limited number of characters: Convict Glancy, Muster-Master Stoneman, Under-Sheriff Ropewell, Chaplain Ford
Setting	One setting at one point in time: penal station in Oatlands, Van Diemen's Land, a September evening in 1837.
Language	Filled with irony (For example, p. 8, ll. 4ff. "Convict Glancy, No 17,927, transportee ex ship Pestonjee [...] will suffer the extreme penalty of the law for having, in an intemperate moment, objected to the mild discipline with which a genial and loving motherland had sought to correct his criminal tendencies")
Suspense	Although Glancy knows that his escape and the murder of the warden will definitely lead to his execution, he finally returns back to the penal station. This surprising turning point reveals the inevitability of a convict's fate in Australia: there is no chance of escaping and no hope of a free and happy life. Although the escape has caused some annoyance among the penal officers, the convict system returns to its daily routine by executing Convict Glancy the next morning.

Characteristics of a short story

Characteristic features of a short story	Definition	Examples from the text
Incident	It centres around one *incident*, which is often revealed as an unusual one.	
Plot	It organizes character and action into a simple plot (*plot stories vs. plotless stories*), focusing on a single turning point or surprising reversal.	
Characters	It concentrates on a limited number of *characters*, often revealing their state of mind at some single moment of crisis and presenting a clash of characters.	
Setting	It is often confined to one *setting* covering in detail only a short period of time.	
Language	It is told in *language* highly charged with meaning and suggestion.	
Suspense	It builds up *suspense* towards the end (dénoue-ment).	

Useful phrases for text analysis:

The short story deals with … /It centres around the question of … /The main topic is …
It describes the situation of … /The constituent elements of the plot are … /The tension emerges in line …/The story reaches its climax in line …
The main characters are …
The short story takes place in … /is set in …
The language is colloquial/formal/includes a lot of slang word /plays with different registers, includes literary devices such as metaphor, simile …

Basic literary terms and stylistic devices

Literary terms

direct characterization: the character is explicitly described and the narrator comments on his/her actions (*telling*).

indirect characterization: the reader must infer what the character is like through his/her outward appearance, speech, thoughts, actions, interaction with and reactions from other characters (*showing*).

A **character** compromises a variety of **dimensions** such as appearance, gender, age, religion, martial status, education, occupation, financial status, hobbies, emotions, motivations, behaviour, fears and a back story.
Characters can either be

- **complex (round)**, meaning that they tend to be major characters who encounter conflict and are changed by it. They tend to be more fully developed and described.
- **flat**, which means that these are usually minor characters who don't undergo substantial change or growth in the course of a story. They usually play a supporting role to the main character.

plot: a series of related events that make up the main story in a book, film etc. A second, less important story in the same book or film is called a subplot. (*what?*)

setting: a particular time or place that a play, book, film or similar happens in (*when? where?*)

point of view: perspective from which the story is told.

- **first person**: a character narrates the story, hence, s/he is part of the plot and has a rather limited perspective on the events
- **omniscient narrator**: knows everything, may reveal the motivations, thoughts and feelings of the characters, and give the reader more information.

Stylistic devices

Term	Definition	Example
Alliteration	Repetition of a sound at the beginning of neighbouring words.	Peter Piper picked a peck of pickled peppers.
Accumulation	Enumeration: a row of similar expressions.	I have dared to love you, wildly, passionately, devotedly, hopelessly. (O. Wilde)
Anaphora	Successive clauses (sentences) starting with the same word.	It was the best of times, it was the worst of times, it was the age of wisdom, it was the age of foolishness. (C. Dickens)
Antithesis	Contrast, opposing words, phrases, structures, characters or views.	It was the best of times, it was the worst of times. (C. Dickens)
Chiasmus	Reversal in the order of words in the two halves of a sentence.	Love's fire heats water, water cools not love. (W. Shakespeare)
Euphemism	Using a polite expression for sth unpleasant.	to pass away (to die), friendly fire (being attacked by your own army)
Hyperbole	Exaggeration, overstatement, making sth better or greater than it is	It was so cold that even the polar bears had to wear jackets.
Metaphor	Poetical comparison without *like* or *as*.	Life is but a walking shadow. (W. Shakespeare)
Oxymoron	Combination of two seemingly contradictory terms (condensed paradox).	Definite maybe/act naturally/pretty ugly
Parallelism	Repeating similar or identical words, phrases, constructions in neighbouring lines, sentences or paragraphs.	If I am occasionally a little overdressed, I make up for it by being always immensely overeducated. (O. Wilde)
Personification	Presenting ideas, objects or animals as persons	a smiling moon
Repetition	Deliberately using a word or phrase more than once.	Tomorrow and tomorrow and tomorrow, creeps in this petty pace from day to day. (W. Shakespeare)
Rhetorical Question	Question to which the answer is obvious.	Don't we all love peace?
Simile	Comparison using *like* or *as*.	A woman without a man is like a fish without a bicycle. (Irina Dunn)
Symbol	Sth concrete (object, character or event) standing for sth abstract.	A dove = peace; a rose = love

1.5 Describing plot and setting in the short story

In der folgenden Stunde sollen die Schülerinnen und Schüler die allgemeine Handlungsstruktur sowie die explizite Darstellung von Raum und Zeit in der *short story* erarbeiten. Für die Darstellung der Handlungsstruktur eignet sich die *Herringbone technique* als *graphic organizer* (vgl. Thaler 2009). Dazu werden die Informationen des Textes den sechs Leitfragen (*Who? When? Why? What? Where? How?*) zugeordnet. Aus der Beantwortung ergibt sich die Hauptinformation des Textes (Tafelbild 1). Diese soll nach dem *Think-Pair-Share*-Prinzip zunächst mit dem Nachbarn abgeglichen und anschließend im Plenum diskutiert werden. Im Hinblick auf die Zeitstruktur sind in der *short story* der Verzicht auf eine umfassende Darstellung des Handlungsortes und eine Vermeidung von häufigen Ortswechseln und längeren Zeitverläufen charakteristisch. In der vorliegenden Geschichte zeigt sich dies an der Beschränkung auf einen Zeitraum von wenigen Stunden zwischen Mitternacht und Morgen des nächsten Tages. Die Schüler sollen mithilfe des Tafelbildes diese Zeitstruktur als Hausaufgabe für die nächste Stunde erarbeiten (Tafelbild 2 – Lösung).

Herringbone technique (graphic organizer)

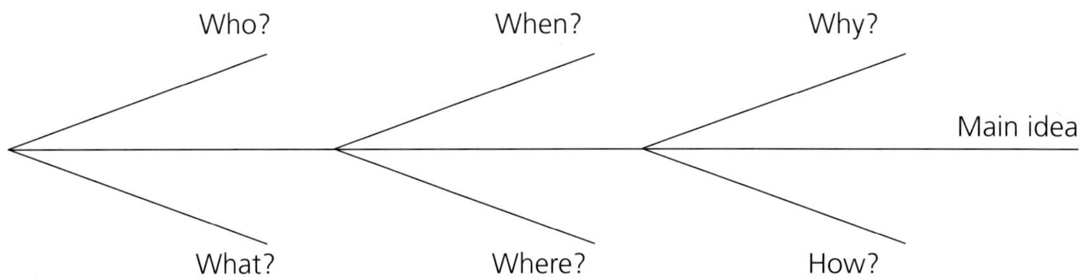

Herringbone technique (Lösung)

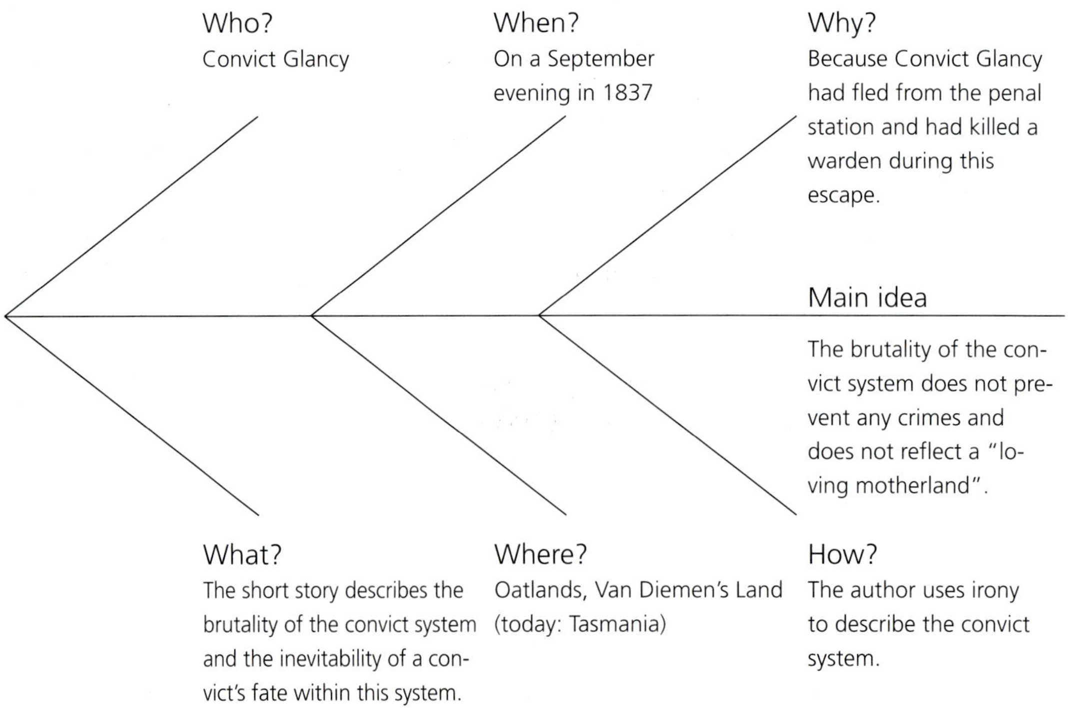

Zeitstruktur: How Muster-Master Stoneman Earned His Breakfast (Lösung)

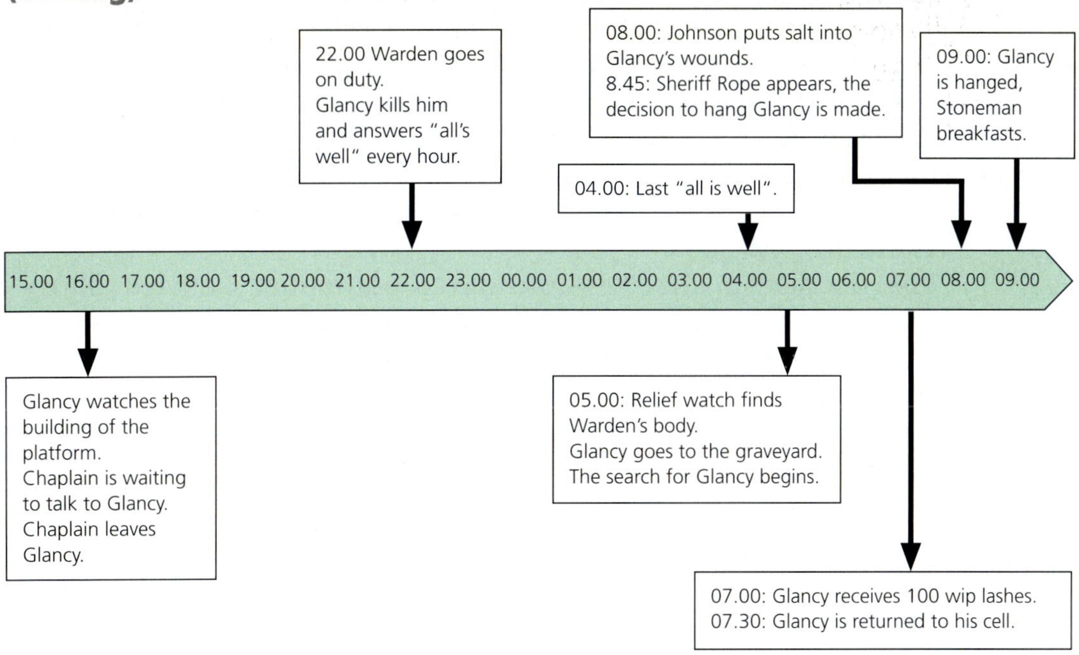

1.6 Focusing on language

Die Leserlenkung durch sprachliche Mittel ist in der vorliegenden Kurzgeschichte von besonderer Bedeutung. Daher soll in der folgenden Stunde insbesondere die Ironie als Mittel herausgearbeitet werden. Durch die kreative Umformung des Textes soll dabei nicht nur die Ironie als Stilmittel deutlich werden, sondern es soll zugleich von den Schülerinnen und Schülern erkannt werden, wie diese Ironie dazu genutzt wird, die Ungerechtigkeit des *convict systems* zu unterstreichen. Dazu sollen sie zunächst die nachfolgenden Textabschnitte erneut lesen und daraufhin einen Textabschnitt so umschreiben, dass alle Formen von Ironie und eigener Meinung herausgestrichen werden und der Text als objektive Darstellung im Rahmen einer Zeitungsmeldung gelten kann. Danach sollen die Schülerinnen und Schüler ihre Ergebnisse untereinander austauschen (*Think-Pair-Share*) und abschließend im Plenum diskutieren. Als Hausaufgabe sollen die Arbeitsergebnisse noch einmal verschriftlicht werden.

The following passages are taken from the short story. Imagine that you have to write a short article for the local newspaper informing your readers about the new convict. Please choose one text and after writing your own text, present it to your classmates and discuss which text seems more effective. What sort of language does the author use to create this effect? What could be the possible reason for the author to use this sort of language or the intended effect?

Text 1 (p. 11):
"At nine o'clock on the following morning, Convict Glancy, No. 17,927, transportee ex ship Pestonjee Bomanjee (second trip), originally under

sentence for seven years for the theft of a silk handkerchief from a London "swell", will suffer the extreme penalty of the law for having, in an intemperate moment, objected to the mild discipline with which a genial and loving motherland had sought to correct his criminal tendencies. In other words, Convict Glancy, metaphorically goaded by the wordy insults and literally by the bayonet-tip of one of his motherland's reformatory agents – to wit, Road-gang Overseer James Jones – had scattered J.J.'s brains over a good six square yards of metalled roadway."

P. Warung, How Muster-Master Stoneman Earned His Breakfast

Text 2 (pp. 12/13):

"This decision of the duly-constituted authorities Convict Glancy has somewhat irrelevantly (as it will seem to us at this enlightened day) acknowledged by a fervent "Thank God!" – an ejaculation rendered the more remarkable by the fact that never before in his convict history had he linked the name of the Deity with any expression of gratitude for the many blessings enjoyed by him in that state of penal servitude to which it had pleased the same Deity to call him. On the contrary, he had constantly indulged in maledictions on his fate and on his Maker. He had resolutely cursed the benignant forces with which the System and the King's Regulations had surrounded him and he had failed to reverence as he ought the triangles, the gang-chains, the hominy, the prodding bayonet, and the other things which would have conducted to his reformation, had he but manifested a more humble and obedient spirit. No wonder, therefore, as Chaplain Ford said, that it has come about that he has qualified for the capital doom."

P. Warung, How Muster-Master Stoneman Earned His Breakfast

Mögliche Schülerantworten:

Oatlands Chronicle

September 5th, 1837

Arrived:

Yesterday morning, Convict Glancy (No. 17,927) arrived in Oatlands goal. Glancy, who had originally been sentenced for seven years for the theft of a handkerchief, had earlier killed one of his overseers, Mr. James Jones in a brutal way.

Reports from court:

Yesterday's court session came with a surprise as the accused, Convict Glancy, commented the imposition of the death penalty with the words "Thank God!". Glancy, who has never shown any gratitude towards the convict system inflicted on him so far and constantly cursed all the measures used against him, such as flogging, being chained together with other convicts and other such disciplinary measures. Chaplain Ford commented Glancy's behavior "No wonder he finally qualified for the death penalty."

1.7 Perspective/author's intention

Den Abschluss der Auseinandersetzung mit der ersten Kurzgeschichte der Sammlung bildet die Analyse der Erzählperspektive. Der Erzählperspektive kommt in allen Kurzgeschichten der vorliegenden Sammlung besondere Bedeutung zu, daher soll diese an dieser Stelle mit

den Schülerinnen und Schülern ausführlicher behandelt und immer wieder ergänzt werden.
Da nach Stanzels typologischer Definition der Erzählperspektive (1995) zwischen Innen- und Außenperspektive, der Einheit von Erzähler und Figur sowie zwischen Erzähler und Reflektorfigur (Person, aus deren Perspektive wir die Handlung wahrnehmen) zu unterscheiden ist, empfehlen Nünning/Surkamp (2008, S. 208) ein mehrschrittiges Vorgehen, bei dem zunächst dem Erzähler der Kurzgeschichte (*Who speaks?*) und in einem zweiten Schritt nach der Perspektive (*Through whose eyes do we see the events?*) gefragt wird.

Who is speaking?
Is he/she present in the story? Does the narrator participate in the story?
What do we get to know about the narrator?

Mögliches Tafelbild:

Who is speaking? – Narrative perspective in the short story

Narrator (≠ author)

A: First-person narrator
A character in the text who uses the first person singular. The character may be a protagonist or just a minor character. The first-person perspective is used to express a character's feelings and experiences. The reader is invited to identify with the first-person narrator.

B: Third-person narrator
The narrator is not part of the narration and uses third person forms ("he", "she" or "they") to refer to the characters.

B1: Omniscient third-person narrator
The narrator has an unlimited point of view, is able to describe the feelings and thoughts of all characters, report on past events and predict future events.

B2: Limited third-person narrator
The narrator has a limited point of view and focuses mainly on the thoughts and feelings of one character (limits themself to one perspective).

Unintrusive ('neutral')
The narrator describes events without much commentary and interpretation of characters' actions and thoughts.

Intrusive
The (omniscient) narrator describes the events and adds further comments on characters actions and thoughts.

Result: the short story *How Muster-Master Stoneman Earned His Breakfast* is told from the perspective of an onmniscient, intrusive third-person narrator.

Die Analyse der ersten Kurzgeschichte ergibt, dass der Erzähler nicht direkt an der Erzählung teilnimmt, sondern als übergeordneter Erzähler fungiert (*superordinate narrator*). Der regelmäßige Sprecherwechsel zwischen direkter Figurenrede zu indirekter Erzählerrede zeigt deutlich diese übergeordnete Stellung des Erzählers. Die Schüler erkennen aus der Kurzgeschichte, dass der Erzähler nicht direkt in das Geschehen eingebunden ist (*first-person narrator*), sondern als auktoriale bzw. personale Erzählinstanz auftritt (*third-person narrator*). Das Tafelbild kann dazu genutzt werden, diesen Erkenntnisprozess der Schüler zu begleiten und sie ggf. zum Auffinden von Belegstellen im Text anzuleiten.

Die nächste Leitfrage zielt auf den Grad der Allgegenwart (*omnipresence*) bzw. Allwissenheit des Erzählers (*omniscience*). Beide Aspekte lassen sich in der Kurzgeschichte leicht erfassen, wenn man nach Informationen über den Erzähler sucht. Da die Kurzgeschichte keinerlei Informationen (wie Alter, Geschlecht, moralische Einstellung) über den Erzähler preisgibt, muss es sich um einen neutralen Erzähler handeln (*covert narrator*). Allerdings tritt der Erzähler an mehreren Stellen auch deutlicher hervor, indem er die Handlung kommentiert und durch eigene Werturteile und Interpretationen erweitert. Besonders deutlich wird dies im Zusammenhang mit den (von den Schülerinnen und Schülern bereits erarbeiteten) Textstellen mit ironischer Prägung. Insbesondere dort, wo das *convict system* dargestellt wird, präsentiert der Erzähler eine eigene Position und fügt durch Mittel der Ironie Werturteile in die Erzählung ein. Aufgrund der wertenden Erzählerrede scheint es sich im vorliegenden Erzähltext um einen auktorialen Erzähler zu handeln. Um dies mit den Schülerinnen und Schülern zu erarbeiten, bieten sich folgende Leitfragen an:

Can you detect any narrational intrusions such as comments, critical remarks or similar?
Does the narrator make any explicit moral comments or judgement?
Can you find examples of the narrator commenting or interpreting the characters' actions and the plot in general?

Text	Type of intrusion	Possible effect on the reader
p. 10, ll. 8f. "Sixteen hours hence that face will look its last upon the world which has stricken it countless cruel blows".	Comment	Creates empathy for the convict behind bars.
p. 11, ll. 5–11: "At nine o'clock ... objected to the mild discipline with which a genial and loving motherland had sought to correct his criminal tendencies."	Irony	To question the form of penalty and the intended effect on the criminal.
p. 12, ll. 12ff. "He had resolutely cursed the benignant forces with which the System and the King's regulation had surrounded him ..."	Irony	The forms of legal punishment, like whipping, flogging, hard work in road gangs, physical torture and others are presented as inhuman and not suitable as coming on the part of a benign and caring sovereign.

Die auktorielle und zugleich wertende Erzählweise ist für viele Erzählungen im 19. Jahrhundert typisch, da durch sie zugleich die Überzeugung verdeutlicht wird, menschliches Verhalten sei nach allgemeingültigen Maßstäben geordnet und ließe sich entsprechend daran messen. Darüber hinaus versucht der Autor, seine Überzeugung von der Ungerechtigkeit des *convict systems* in dieser Erzählweise darzustellen und sie damit in das allgemeine Wertesystem einzuordnen. Die insbesondere durch Elemente der Ironie ausgedrückte Ablehnung des *convict systems* wird entsprechend nicht nur als individuelle, personale Sichtweise einer einzelnen Figur der Geschichte ausgedrückt, sondern erhält durch die gewählte Erzählweise zugleich auktorielle Züge, d.h. wird als allgemeingültig und verbindliche Sichtweise der Gesellschaft dargestellt.
Um abschließend den Schülerinnen und Schülern zu vermitteln, wie eine personale Erzählperspektive die gesamte Erzählsituation beeinflusst und in der Wirkung verändert, sollen die Schüler in einer zusammenfassenden Hausaufgabe einen Dialog zwischen Glancy und dem Priester Ford verfassen. Indem dieser Dialog aus der Erzählperspektive des Geistlichen verfasst wird, ändert sich die Wirkung auf den Leser. Die von Glancy vorgebrachten Klagen und Beschwerden klingen weniger glaubwürdig und könnten als ungerechtfertigtes Hadern eines Kriminellen mit dem (unvermeidlichen) Schicksal verstanden werden.

In his final minutes before the execution takes place, Glancy once again has a short discussion with Chaplain Ford. Write down the dialogue, in which Glancy complains about the injustice of the convict system, from Chaplain Ford's perspective.

1.8 Project work – Ideas and suggestions

Die Behandlung der Kurzgeschichte *How Muster-Master Stoneman Earned His Breakfast* ist komplex und erfordert ein umfassendes Kontextwissen zum *convict system*. Alternativ zu dem oben genannten Vorgehen oder als vertiefende Aktivität bzw. als Thema für Fach- und Projektarbeiten können Schülerinnen zu folgenden Themen eigenständig arbeiten:

1. Prison systems all around the world
2. The death penalty – then and now
3. Famous Australian convicts

Component 2

The Australian Outback – Shaping Australian identity?

2.1 "Man constantly battles against the elements" – Life in the Australian bush

Im Gegensatz zum ersten *Component,* bei dem vor allem die Frage im Vordergrund stand, ob und wie die Einwanderergruppe der *convicts* zur Entwicklung australischer Identität beigetragen haben (soziale Identität), soll in *Component 2* die Frage aufgeworfen werden, wie das Land selbst auf die Identitätsbildung eingewirkt hat (Ortsidentität). Gerade das australische Outback hat dabei seit der Zeit der frühen Siedler eine besondere Rolle gespielt und wirkt bis in die Gegenwart auf das australische Selbstverständnis ein.
Dazu hat in erheblichem Maße auch das Gemälde *The Drover's Wife* (1945) von Russell Drysdale (1912–1981) beigetragen. Das Gemälde, das heute in der *National Gallery of Australia* in Canberra zu sehen ist, zeigt eine Frau in mittlerem Alter mit einfachem braunen Kleid und schwarzem Hut. Ihr ausdrucksloses Gesicht in Richtung des Betrachters gewandt, scheint sie auf etwas oder jemanden zu warten. Neben der Frau, die in der linken Hand eine Reisetasche trägt, kann der Betrachter im Bildhintergrund einen Planwagen sowie eine zweite Person erkennen, die offensichtlich das Vieh versorgt. Die Gegend wirkt trostlos, das vertrocknete Land bietet weder für Mensch noch für das Vieh geeignete Lebensbedingungen.
Der Kunstkritiker Paul Haefliger sieht daher in Drysdale's Bild vor allem eine Allegorie auf die schwierigen Lebensumstände im australischen Outback: „[Drysdale] conveys a difficult and lonely existence, where man constantly battles against the elements" (Sydney Morning Herald, 23. Januar 1948, S. 2).
Durch vertiefte Bildanalyse sollen die Schülerinnen und Schüler diese Sicht auf das australische Outback herausarbeiten und in einem späteren Schritt mit alternativen Sichtweisen auf das Leben im Busch kontrastieren.
In einem ersten Schritt sollen sie dazu das Bild möglichst detailgenau beschreiben. Dazu sollen sie zunächst auf die Figur der Frau fokussieren und sich Notizen zu Kleidung, Gestik und Mimik der Frau machen. Anschließend sollen sie diese Ergebnisse mit einem Mitschüler vergleichen. In einem weiteren Schritt sollen sie dann den Hintergrund des Bildes näher beschreiben und dazu Vermutungen über die Lebensbedingungen im Outback anstellen.

1. Describe the woman in the painting. Try to find as many details as possible and then share your ideas with your partner.
2. Describe the landscape. What additional items can you see? What can you say about spatial relationships (… in the foreground/… the background)?
3. What does Drysdale's painting reveal about living conditions in the Australian outback?

Russell Drysdale: The Drover's Wife (1945)

Sir Russell Drysdale (1912–1981) was an Australian artist who was influenced by abstract and surrealist art and has become famous for his own interpretation of remote Australian landscapes. His painting, *The Drover's Wife* (1945), is part of a series of paintings that focused on the effects of the drought in western New South Wales. While near Deniliquin in the south-west of the state, he made a drawing of two victims of the 1944 drought, a drover and his wife with their wagon, on which he later based this painting. The title 'The Drover's Wife' had already been used for a short story by the Australian writer Henry Lawson in 1892. Both the short story and the painting have since inspired more recent writers like Murray Bail, Barbara Jefferis and Frank Moorhouse to continue the narration of 'the drover's wife'.

Assignments

1. Describe the woman in the painting. Try to find as many details as possible and then share your ideas with your partner.

	You	Your neighbour
headwear		
dress		
accessories		
posture		
facial expression		
arms and hands		
legs and feet		

2. Describe the landscape. What additional items can you see? What can you say about spatial relationships (… in the foreground/… the background)?
3. What does Drysdale's painting reveal about living conditions in the Australian outback?

Lösungsvorschlag zu *Copy 9*:

1.

headwear	black hat, worn-out
dress	brown dress
accessories	handbag
posture	relaxed, tired, looks a bit like a monument (looks down on the viewer), appears to be patient and independent
facial expression	seems to be looking out quietly with steady eyes, firm mouth
arms and hands	Her arms hang down loosely, one hand firmly holds her large handbag.
legs and feet	Her feet almost touch the lower margin of the painting, turned towards the horse-drawn wagon.

2.
- The landscape is devastated (probably after a drought), the (few) trees are bare-branched, the soil is burnt and does not show any signs of life. In the background, one can see a coach, drawn by horses and a second person, probably the woman's husband who seems to be feeding the horses.
- There is a spatial distance between the woman and her husband, which might also indicate some kind of tension between them. She does not rely on her husband or seeks his company but stands further away from him, looking in a different direction (the viewer's direction).

3.
- Drysdale's painting shows a strong, self-confident woman who is probably been forced to leave her own piece of land in the Australian Outback because of the drought.
- The leafless trees and the brown soil show that a livelihood in the hostile and depressing environment of the outback seems nearly impossible.
- Her facial expression, however, underlines her determination to stay (while her husband has probably already given up and is now preparing the horses to leave).
- The painting can be seen as in praise of the settlers (and especially their women) who successfully endured the hardships of the Australian outback.

Als Hausaufgabe sollen die Schülerinnen und Schüler einen Brief aus der Sicht der Frau verfassen, in dem sie ihrer Schwester in Sydney über das Leben im Outback berichtet. Im Brief sollten noch einmal wesentliche Aspekte der Bildanalyse aufgegriffen und durch Perspektivwechsel für die Schülerinnen und Schüler erfahrbar gemacht werden.

Write a short letter in which you write to your sister in Sydney about living conditions in the outback.

Individuelle Lösungen.

2.2 Waltzing Matilda – Australia's unofficial national anthem

A. B. (Banjo) Patterson's Song über einen *swagman*, der sich auf der Walz im australischen Outback befindet, gilt bis heute als Australiens heimliche Nationalhymne und hat die australische Identität wesentlich mit geprägt. Zugleich wird durch die Auseinandersetzung der Schülerinnen und Schüler mit dem bekanntesten australischen Volkslied eine Brücke geschlagen zur Kurzgeschichte *How Muster-Master Stoneman Earned His Breakfast* aus *Component 1*, deren Protagonist ebenfalls gegen das Gesetz verstoßen hat und schließlich zu Tode kommt.
Im Rahmen der Analyse wird inhaltlich die Frage aufgeworfen, wieso eine Geschichte mit solch tragischer Handlung zur heimlichen Nationalhymne der Australier werden konnte und sich bis heute solcher Popularität erfreut. Um der Frage nachzugehen, sollen die Schüler zunächst in einem ersten Schritt den *swagman* und seinen Alltag beschreiben. Dazu erhalten sie den Liedtext (***Copy 12***) und sammeln Informationen im Text zum *swagman*. Anschließend wird das Tafelbild auf die übrigen Charaktere ausgedehnt.

1. Describe the main characters and their living conditions in the Australian outback as described in the song

The swagman	• a temporary worker • travels by foot from farm to farm • carries his swag (a waterproof bedroll) and leads a solitary life • is proud and self-sufficient • defies authority in the end by preferring suicide to being arrested by the police
The squatter	• landowner and owner of the animal illegally taken by the swagman • relies on the police to get back what belongs to him • wants the swagman to be arrested for his theft
The police	• try to maintain law and order in the remote areas of the outback • support the landowners and are about to arrest the swagman

2. Why do you think the swagman calls Matilda his "darling"?

Matilda is the swag used by pioneers who were settling the Australian outback. The swag is their only travelling companion and their home at night, at the same time. Therefore, it is very dear to them.

3. Why does the swagman commit suicide in the end?

The swagman in the story gets ready for his afternoon tea and at first seems lucky as well, as a sheep crosses his path promising a substantial meal for him that night. As the sheep's owner approaches the farm-hand together with the police, his only escape is the deep water nearby where he unfortunately gets drowned. In this way, at least the authorities cannot arrest him for his theft.

4. Why do you suppose the story of the swagman in *Waltzing Matilda* is so popular among Australians?

The average Australian's attitude towards authority is one of defiance. This can be seen in the fate of the bushman who, instead of being confronted with the police and the consequences of his theft, preferred to kill himself. His story has been an all-time favourite, going back to the beginnings of Australian white settlement when convicts suffered under the privations of a penal colony. Hence, a distrust of rules and authority and whoever represents these seems to be engrained in the *national character*. The song represents this *national character* and serves as a reminder of the early period of settlement which Australians are very proud of. The popularity of *Waltzing Matilda* is to some extend ambiguous: On the one hand, it is closely linked to the early settlement of Australia in the 18th/19th century, on the other hand the song about a temporary worker who steals a sheep and drowns himself in order to avoid being arrested by the police seems a bit unsuitable for a national anthem. However, the song's popularity is partly based on the fact that Australians have always been on the side of the underdogs and independent rovers.

In einem zweiten Schritt sollen die Schülerinnen und Schüler sich intensiver mit der Rezeption des Liedes auseinandersetzen und dazu in Gruppen weitere Informationen zusammentragen. Für die Gruppenrecherche ist ein Internetzugang erforderlich – die Gruppenarbeit kann aber auch von den Schülern arbeitsteilig als Hausaufgabe bearbeitet werden. Für die Behandlung der Kurzgeschichte *A Drover's Wife* ist die Gruppenarbeit allerdings nicht erforderlich und kann bei Bedarf auch entfallen.

A. B. Paterson: Waltzing Matilda (1895)

Oh there was once a swagman camped in the billabongs,
Under the shade of a Coolibah tree;
And he sang as he looked at the old billy boiling,
'Who'll come a-waltzing Matilda with me.'

Who'll come a-waltzing Matilda, my darling,
Who'll come a-waltzing Matilda with me.
Waltzing Matilda and leading a water-bag,
Who'll come a-waltzing Matilda with me.

Up came the jumbuck to drink at the waterhole,
Up jumped the swagman and grabbed him in glee;
And he sang as he put him away in his tucker-bag,
'You'll come a-waltzing Matilda with me.'

CHORUS

Up came the squatter a-riding his thoroughbred;
Up came policemen – one, two and three.
'Whose is the jumbuck you've got in the tucker bag?
You'll come a-waltzing Matilda with we.'

CHORUS

Up sprang the swagman and jumped in the waterhole,
Drowning himself by the Coolibah tree;
And his voice can be heard as it sings in the billabongs,
'Who'll come a-waltzing Matilda with me?'

CHORUS

Text and music: trad.

billabong a branch of a river forming a backwater or stagnant pool
Coolibah tree Australian gum tree
billy a tin or enamel cooking pot
waltzing Matilda carry a bundle of personal belongings
Matilda a bushman's bundle of personal belongings
jumbuck a sheep
glee great delight
tucker-bag a food storage bag

squatter a large-scale sheep or cattle farmer
thoroughbred a horse of pure breed

swagman a man carrying a bundle of personal belongings

Waltzing Matilda – Group activity

In small groups, select one of the following tasks to research. You will need access to a computer first of all and then to present your findings clearly to the rest of the class.

Group 1: The song and its content

Task:
Create a poster which explains the background history of the song and explains the differences in the various versions. Present your poster to the rest of the class.

Use the website http://www.matildacentre.com.au/web/matilda-centre/the-song to work out the background and the origins of the song. When and where was the song written and where did the tune originate?

The song quickly became part of Australia's oral tradition. However, there is more than one version of the song. There are at least three main streams of 'Waltzing Matilda': the Macpherson/Paterson version (1895), the Cowan version (c.1903) and a third, oral version (the Queensland version). Some information can be found at
http://en.wikipedia.org/wiki/Waltzing_Matilda
and
http://www.nla.gov.au/epubs/waltzingmatilda/2–Versions.html s.u.

Group 2: The song and its composer

Task:
Prepare a short dialogue in which the author Paterson is being interviewed by a reporter and reveals some information about his life and the circumstances of the song's development. Present your dialogue to the class.

Use the website http://dl.screenaustralia.gov.au/module/207/ to find out about the poet who wrote the song.
What do we learn about the writer A. B. (Banjo) Paterson and how he wrote the song?
Additional information about Banjo Paterson can be found at http://resources.news.com.au/files/2009/08/05/1225758/303939-dt-classmate-file-banjo-patterson.pdf
and
http://www.wallisandmatilda.com.au/banjo-paterson-biography.shtml.

Group 3: The song and its (political) context

Task:
Prepare a short debate in which you explain and discuss the possible link between the folk song and the political uprising of 1891. Enact your debate in class.

Use the website www.nla.gov.au/epubs/waltzingmatilda/ to find out the meaning behind the song. Some people talk about the shearer's strikes of the 1890s and think that this song is a political protest against the squatters and their treatment of the shearers. What do you think? Justify your response based on your research.

Additional information can be found at
http://en.wikipedia.org/wiki/1891_Australian_shearers'_strike,
http://www.abc.net.au/news/stories/2010/02/12/2818131.htm
and
http://www.suite101.com/content/waltzing-matilda-lyrics-andrew-banjo-paterson-a94034.

Group 4: The song and its use as unofficial anthem

Task:
Prepare a leaflet in which you vote for *Waltzing Mathilda* as the official national anthem. Explain why the song is more popular/more suitable than the National Anthem 'Advance Australia Fair' and present your arguments to the class.

Use this website to uncover the story behind the Australian National Anthem: http://www.nla.gov.au/epubs/waltzingmatilda/4-Anthem-Choosing.html.
What is an anthem? Which one do we now use? Is this representative of all Australia?
What other anthems were considered for Australia's National Anthem? Which one does your group prefer? Why?

Additional information can be found at
http://en.wikipedia.org/wiki/Australian_plebiscite,_1977_(National_Song)
and
http://www.dfat.gov.au/facts/national_anthem.pdf.

Additional resources the groups might find helpful:
- http://www.matildacentre.com.au
- http://www.nla.gov.au/epubs/waltzingmatilda/
- http://knol.google.com/k/waltzing-matilda-australia-s-national-song
- http://dl.screenaustralia.gov.au/module/207/
- http://resources.news.com.au/files/2009/08/05/1225758/303939-dt-classmate-file-banjo-patterson.pdf

2.3 The Drover's Wife (1892) – Henry Lawson

Die *pre-reading activity* knüpft an die Bildbetrachtung an und sammelt noch einmal wichtige Aspekte des Lebens im Outback, die die Schülerinnen und Schüler im Rahmen der Hausaufgabe formuliert haben. Um für einen zügigen Ablauf zu sorgen, kann zunächst das Grundgerüst (s. u.) vorgestellt werden. Die Schülerinnen und Schüler können in Partnerarbeit und durch Vergleich der zu Hause erstellten Texte ihre eigenen Versionen erstellen, die dann im Plenum besprochen und von dem Lehrer an der Tafel zusammengefasst werden.

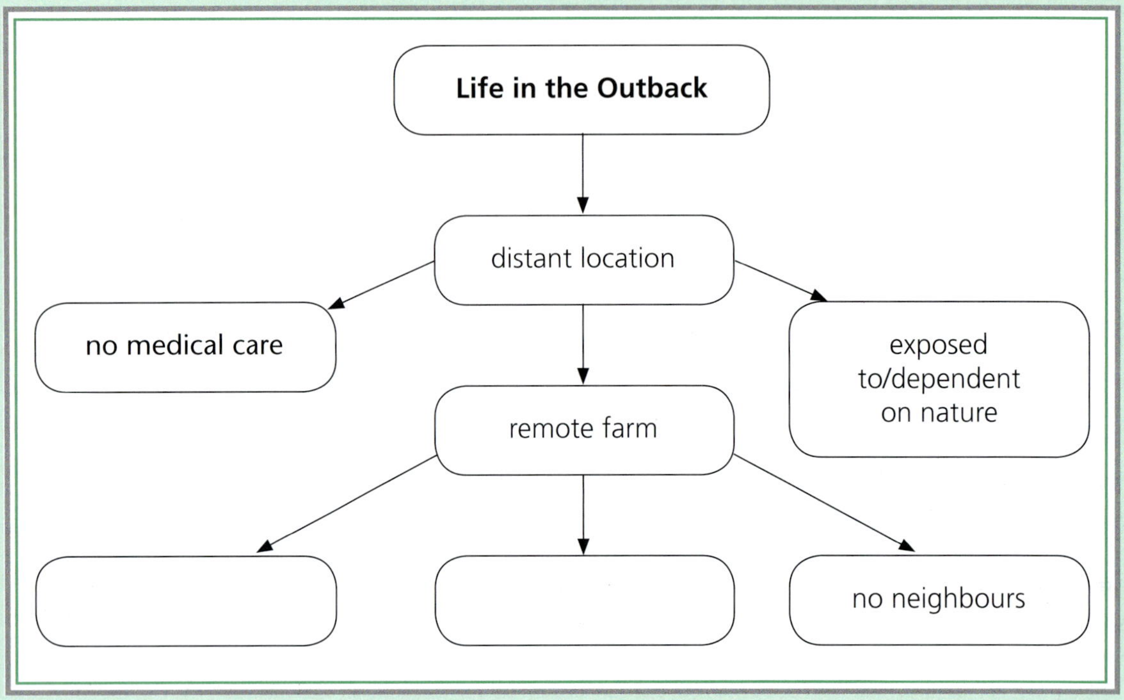

Das Tafelbild kann, je nach Schülerbeiträgen, durch folgende Aspekte ergänzt werden:

hardly any social life, trust amongst family members and employers essential, no schooling – limited future options for children, poor living conditions, fear of animals, droughts as a threat to survival, physical hardship, loneliness, isolation

Nach der *pre-reading activity* wird mit den Schülerinnen und Schülern der erste Abschnitt der *short story* (bis S. 29, Z. 18 „... that blinded snake.") gemeinsam gelesen.

1. Which of your expectations get further support from the text? What does the text reveal about the living conditions in the Australian outback? Share your results with your partner. Which similarities or differences can you find?

• poor living conditions	p. 27, ll. 1 f.: "two-roomed house made of timber and slabs"
• loneliness and isolation	p. 27, l. 4: "Bush all round ... Nineteen miles to the nearest sign of civilisation ..."
• fear of animals	p. 27, ll. 13 ff. "Snake! Mother, here's a snake"

Abschließend wird der nachfolgende Impuls mit den Schülerinnen und Schülern diskutiert, wodurch zugleich die wesentlichen Merkmale zum *setting* zusammengefasst werden:

2. Which function does the setting of the story have? Is it important for the narration or can it be easily changed? How is it described in the text?

   The remote setting in the Australian outback is a distinctive element of the story and is therefore highly relevant for the narration. It is described as endless, flat with bush all around the house and nothing of importance within eyesight.

2.4 Annäherungen an den Text: Reziprokes Lesen

Durch die Methode des reziproken Lesens sollen die Schülerinnen und Schüler die *short story A drover's wife* weitgehend selbstständig erschließen und dabei systematisch Kompetenzen zum Textverständnis entwickeln (vgl. Brüning/Saum 2009: 102 ff.).
Der Text wird dazu in vier (etwa gleich große) Sinnabschnitte aufgeteilt, die von den Gruppen schrittweise erarbeitet werden. Folgende Aufteilung des Textes wird vorgeschlagen:

1. Abschnitt: p. 29, l. 19 – p. 32, l. 16
2. Abschnitt: p. 32, l. 17 – p. 35, l. 19
3. Abschnitt: p. 35, l. 20 – p. 37, l. 19
4. Abschnitt: p. 37, l. 20 – p. 39, l. 14

Die Schülerinnen und Schüler werden zu Beginn der Stunde in Kleingruppen mit jeweils vier Teilnehmern eingeteilt. Jeder Schüler erhält eine Rollenkarte (A–D), die ihr/ihm eine klare Aufgabe zuweist.
Nach einer kurzen Phase der Einzelarbeit, in der jede Schülerin/jeder Schüler den ersten Textabschnitt liest, sollen in der folgenden Phase der Kooperation verschiedene Aufgaben übernommen werden: Während der erste Schüler A Fragen zum Textabschnitt stellen soll, die von den anderen mithilfe des Textes beantwortet werden, soll Schüler B den Textabschnitt sinnvoll zusammenfassen, Schüler C Erklärungen unklarer Textstellen beisteuern und Schüler D schließlich vorhersagen, was wohl im kommenden Abschnitt passieren wird. Daran schließt sich eine erneute Phase der Stillarbeit an, in der der nächste Textabschnitt gelesen wird, bevor schließlich eine erneute Phase der Kooperation folgt. Dabei werden die Rollenkarten im Uhrzeigersinn weitergereicht, sodass schließlich im Verlauf des Leseprozesses alle Schüler einmal die verschiedenen Rollen übernommen haben.
Neben Wörterbüchern und Kopien der Textabschnitte sollten die Schülerinnen und Schüler in den Arbeitsgruppen Textmarker, Stifte und ausreichend Papier zur Verfügung gestellt bekommen, damit die Textabschnitte auch gemeinsam bearbeitet werden können.

Group reading (reciprocal reading)

Role card A: Asking questions

It is your task to ask questions that can easily be answered after reading the text passage (start with questions like who? when? where? what? and why?). By asking questions, you help your team to find out whether they have understood the central elements of the text passage. Therefore, make sure that you focus on central questions and not on irrelevant details which are not necessary to fully understand the text.

Role card B: Summarizing main ideas

You help your group to understand the text by summarizing the main ideas. Try to concentrate on the essentials and leave out all unnecessary details. Present your summary to the group and ask for corrections and additions.

Role card C: Clarifying difficult text passages

Some text passages may contain difficult elements. Help your group by looking up difficult words in a dictionary and try to paraphrase complex sentences. Discuss difficult passages with your group and try to give meaning to them by having a closer look at the context and deducing meaning from it.

Role card D: Predicting next text passages

Contribute to the collaborative text analysis by predicting how the story might go on. Can you detect open questions that should be answered in the next text passage? Present your ideas to the group and discuss them with your partners.

Als Hausaufgabe werden die Schülerinnen und Schüler gebeten, auf Basis ihrer Gruppenergebnisse eine *summary* zur Kurzgeschichte zu erstellen.

2.5 Describing characters

Nachdem die wesentlichen Merkmale der *short story* mit Bezug auf *plot* und *setting* durch die Methode des reziproken Lesens von den Schülerinnen und Schülern bereits bearbeitet wurden, sollen in dieser Stunde die Hauptfiguren im Zentrum des Unterrichtsgeschehens stehen. Dazu wird noch einmal das Verfahren der Charakterisierung mit den Schülerinnen und Schülern systematisch eingeübt (vgl. Thaler 2009, S. 35 ff.). In einem *Think-Pair-Share*-Verfahren bearbeiten die Schülerinnen und Schüler die nachfolgende Aufgabe zunächst selbstständig, um sie dann mit dem Partner abzugleichen und schließlich im Plenum vorzustellen. Das Arbeitsblatt ***(Copy 13)*** dient der Unterstützung während der Partnerarbeitsphase, wird aber an späterer Stelle noch einmal aufgegriffen (vgl. *Component 3*).

What is the main character like? How does the author tell us about her? Find words, expressions or passages in the text to illustrate this. After filling out the grid, share your results with your partner.

	The protagonist: the woman	
	Your own description	**Quotation**
outward appearance	thin, sun-browned woman	p. 28, l. 1 "The gaunt, sun-browned bushwoman dashes from the kitchen ..."
situation/ position	She is a mother of five, who has to constantly battle the elements (e.g. a bush fire threatening to burn down her house, a flood which had ruined an important dam, a cow disease that threatened her livestock, a mad bullock who had besieged the house for a day, crows and eagles that hunt down her chicken). In addition to this, she has to regularly defend herself against dishonest sundowners and swagmen passing by her house.	p. 33, ll. 9 f. "The rain will make the grass grow, and this reminds her of how she fought a bush fire once while her husband was away." p. 34, ll. 5 f. "She thinks how she fought a flood during her husband's absence." p. 34, ll. 12 f. "She also fought the pleuropneumonia – dosed and bled the remaining cattle, and wept again when her two best cows died." p. 34, ll. 15 "Again, she fought a mad bullock that besieged the house for a day." p. 34, ll. 17 f. "She also fights the crows and eagles that have designed on her chickens." p. 35, ll. 4 f. "Occasionally a bushman in the horrors, or a villainous-looking sundowner, comes and nearly scares the life out of her." p. 35, ll. 9 f. "Only last week a gallows-faced swagman – having satisfied himself that there were no men on the place – threw his swag down on the veranda, and demanded tucker."

	The protagonist: the woman	
	Your own description	**Quotation**
behaviour	The harsh life in the outback has made her tough and very strong. She is a courageous woman (although a bit nerve-shaken recently) who protects her children. Despite her rather sad life in the bush, she still keeps her links to civilization by dressing and tidying her children on Sundays and having a walk with them along the bush-track, just as if she was walking down the streets in the city. Is not used to show any emotions.	p. 31, l. 8 "She is not a coward, but recent events have shaken her nerves." p. 35, ll. 21 f. "All days are much the same to her; but on Sunday afternoon she dresses herself, tidies the children, smartens up baby, and goes for a lonely walk along the bush-track, pushing an old perambulator in front of her." p. 36, ll. 16f. "Her surroundings are not favourable to the development of the "womanly" or sentimental side of her nature."
feelings/ attitudes	She feels a bit nervous about her husband, from whom she has not heard for six months. All her dreams and hopes she had as a young girl have left her; she has become used to being left alone. Has strong feelings for her children and is able to express them.	p. 31, l. 9 "Besides, she has not heard from her husband for six months" p. 31, ll. 19f. "She is used to being left alone. She once lived like this for eighteen months. As a girl she built the usual castles in the air; but all her girlish hopes and aspirations have long been dead." p. 39, ll. 13f. "And she hugs him to her worn-out breast and kisses him; and they sit thus together while the sickly daylight breaks over the bush."
relationship to others	When her husband returns, she does not show any emotions. The bushwoman loves her children above all, but has no time to show it. The children have a very harsh impression of her.	p. 36, l. 12 "She is glad when her husband returns, but she does not gush or make a fuss about it. She gets him something good to eat, and tidies up the children." p. 36, ll. 15f. "She seems contented with her lot. She loves her children, but has no time to show it. She seems harsh to them."

Die Hausaufgabe für die nächste Stunde besteht in dem Schreiben einer Charakterisierung.

Write a portrait of the main character in *The Drover's Wife*. Back up your description with references to the text.

The wife in the short story *A Drover's Wife* by Henry Lawson is presented as a strong, independent woman who is able to battle the elements – a bush fire threatening to burn down her house (p. 33, ll. 9f.), a flood (p. 34, ll. 5), cow disease (p. 34, l. 12), a mad bullock (p. 34, l. 15), crows and eagles that hunt down her chicken (p. 34, l. 17) and can successfully defend herself against dishonest sundowners and swagmen passing by her house (p. 35, ll. 4ff.). All these struggles seem to make her even stronger. She has more or less given up her femininity, because "her surroundings are not favourable to the development of the "womanly" or sentimental side of her nature" (p. 36, ll. 16f.). Her only pleasure is the reading of the "Young Ladies' Journal", which reminds her of the dreams she had as a girl that never came true.

Despite her rather harsh life and her tough appearance, the drover's wife is a sensitive and expressive person. Every time her husband returns, the woman is very happy. However, she does not gush or make a fuss about it (p. 36, l. 12). She usually gets him something good to eat and tidies up the children. In a similar way, the bushwoman loves her children, but is again not able to show it (p. 36, ll. 14f.). However, when a dam breaks (a dam her husband had erected, p. 34, ll. 9f.), she starts crying, as there are still some things, a bushwoman cannot do (p. 34, l. 7). When she finally kills the snake at the end of the story, she is overwhelmed by her feelings and begins to weep (p. 39, l. 10). Her eldest son, realizing that her suffering is mainly caused by his father's absence, promises her not to start a drover's life when he gets older (p. 39, l. 12).

Writing a characterization

Characterization:
direct characterization: the character is explicitly described and the narrator comments on his/her actions (*telling*).
indirect characterization: the reader must infer what the character is like through his/her outward appearance, speech, thoughts, actions, interaction with and reactions from other characters (*showing*).
A character compromises a variety of **dimensions** such as appearance, gender, age, religion, marital status, education, occupation, financial status, hobbies, emotions, motivations, behaviour, fears and a back story.
Characters can either be:

- **complex (round)**, who tend to be major characters encountering conflict and are changed by it. They tend to be more fully developed and described.
- **flat,** which means that these are usually minor characters who don't undergo substantial change or growth in the course of a story. They usually play a supporting role to the main character.

How to write a characterization:

1. Read the text carefully again.
2. Highlight all passages that contain relevant information about your character in the same colour.
3. Describe the character in your own words (fill out the left column).
4. Find passages in the text that underline your description (the highlighted passages in the text).

The following questions are helpful in describing a character:

- Is she/he a main (protagonist, hero/heroine), intermediate or background character?
- Does the character remain stable throughout the story (static) or does she/he change (dynamic character)?
- Is she/he defined by a single quality (flat character, type) or is she/he a complex individual (round character)?

	The protagonist: the woman	
	Your own description:	**Quotation:**
outward appearance		
situation/ position		
behaviour		
feelings/ attitudes		
relationship to others		

2.6 The Bulletin Debate (1892) – Varying perspectives on Australia's Outback

Durch *Component 2* sollte den Schülerinnen und Schülern die Bedeutung des Lebensraums für die australische Identität verdeutlicht werden. Nur vor diesem Hintergrund erschließt sich die besondere Bedeutung der Kurzgeschichte *A Drover's Wife*; sie erhebt die Protagonistin zu einer besonderen Identifikationsfigur, die aber namenlos bleibt und somit auf alle frühen Siedler übertragen werden kann.
Um die besondere Rolle des Outback für die australische Identität genauer zu analysieren, kann abschließend anhand einer historischen Debatte, die zwischen A. B. Paterson und Henry Lawson im Rahmen des Magazins *The Bulletin* in den Jahren 1892–1896 geführt wurde und in die sich weitere Autoren eingemischt haben, nachgezeichnet werden. Im Kern geht es in dem öffentlich geführten Streitgespräch um die Frage, ob das „wahre" Australien eher in den rasant wachsenden Städten an der Küste oder eher im australischen Outback zu finden sei.

Den Auftakt macht dabei ein Gedicht von Henry Lawson (*Up the Country*), in dem er sich gegen eine romantisierende Sicht auf das Leben im Outback wendet, wogegen schließlich A. B. Paterson, der Autor des bekannten Liedes *Waltzing Matilda*, eine Gegenrede entwirft. In seinem Gedicht *In Defense of the Bush* spricht er Lawson direkt an (Z. 1: „So you're back from up the country, Mister Lawson, where you went") und stellt das romantische Leben der *drover* dem hektischen und langweiligen Leben in der Stadt gegenüber.
Die beiden gegensätzlichen Texte sollen von den Schülerinnen und Schülern in Form der strukturierten Kontroverse erarbeitet werden. Die strukturierte Kontroverse (vgl. Brüning/Saum 2008:22) ermöglicht dabei den Austausch von Informationen in Kleingruppen und ermöglicht zugleich den Schülerinnen und Schülern, Argumente zu gegensätzlichen Positionen zu sammeln und zu einem eigenen, begründeten Standpunkt zu gelangen.
Den Ausgangspunkt für die strukturierte Kontroverse liefert die Streitfrage:

> Is it better to live in a city or is it more preferable to live in the country?

Zur Einstimmung in die Diskussion kann eine Vier-Ecken-Methode durchgeführt werden. Dazu sollen sich die Schülerinnen und Schüler in eine der vier Ecken des Raumes begeben, die ihrer persönlichen Meinung entspricht:

> (a) I prefer to live in a big city.
> (b) I prefer to live in the country.
> (c) I am still undecided, but tend more towards living in the city.
> (d) I am still undecided, but tend more towards living in the country.

Anschließend werden die Schülerinnen und Schüler in Vierergruppen eingeteilt, von denen jeweils zwei Partner mithilfe des Textes *Up the country* von Henry Lawson Argumente für das Leben in der Stadt sammeln, die anderen beiden Partner mithilfe des Textes *In Defense of the Bush* Argumente für das Leben im Outback zusammentragen.
In einem ersten Schritt soll jeder Schüler den jeweiligen Text individuell bearbeiten, um dann in einem zweiten Schritt die Argumente mit dem Partner auszutauschen und gemeinsam eine überzeugende Argumentation vorzubereiten. In dieser Erarbeitungsphase sollen auch Verständnisfragen mit dem Partner geklärt werden. Daher ist es sinnvoll, die Gruppen entsprechend mit Wörterbüchern auszustatten.
In der Präsentationsphase stellen die Gruppen ihre Argumente dem anderen Paar in strukturierter Weise vor, während diese die Argumente notieren. Die vortragende Gruppe darf

dabei allerdings nicht unterbrochen werden. Nach Abschluss der jeweiligen Präsentation dürfen jedoch Verständnisfragen gestellt werden.

In einem nächsten Schritt überlegen sich die Gruppen Probleme und Widersprüche in der Argumentation der anderen Partnergruppe und erarbeiten dazu Gegenargumente.
Jetzt wechseln die Paare ihre Positionen (dazu sollte auch der Sitzplatz getauscht werden). Sie müssen nun die jeweils andere Seite vertreten, indem sie zunächst eine Argumentation entwickeln, die möglichst die vorher gefundenen Widersprüche und Probleme aufhebt. Diese Argumentation wird zunächst wieder mit dem Partner besprochen und anschließend der anderen Gruppe vorgestellt.

In einem letzten Schritt dürfen sich die Schülerinnen und Schüler nun von den Textvorgaben lösen und können eigene Argumente und Sichtweisen einbringen.
Nach Abschluss der Kontroverse kann erneut die Vier-Ecken-Methode eingesetzt werden, um Meinungsänderungen und Verschiebungen innerhalb der Klasse deutlich zu machen.

Living in the city vs. living in the Outback – A debate (A)

Please read the following text and collect arguments for a life in the city. Share your ideas with your partner. As a team, try to convince the other group why it is more preferable to live in a city than to live in the country.

a) Henry Lawson: Up the country

I am back from up the country – very sorry that I went –
Seeking for the Southern poets' land whereon to pitch my tent;
I have lost a lot of idols, which were broken on the track,
Burnt a lot of fancy verses, and I'm glad that I am back.
Further out may be the pleasant scenes of which our poets boast,
But I think the country's rather more inviting round the coast.
Anyway, I'll stay at present at a boarding-house in town,
Drinking beer and lemon-squashes, taking baths and cooling down.

'Sunny plains'! Great Scott! – those burning
wastes of barren soil and sand
With their everlasting fences stretching out across the land!
Desolation where the crow is! Desert where the eagle flies,
Paddocks where the luny bullock starts and stares with reddened eyes;
Where, in clouds of dust enveloped, roasted bullock-drivers creep
Slowly past the sun-dried shepherd dragged behind his crawling sheep.
Stunted peak of granite gleaming, glaring like a molten mass
Turned from some infernal furnace on a plain devoid of grass.

Miles and miles of thirsty gutters – strings of muddy water-holes
In the place of `shining rivers' – 'walled by cliffs and forest boles.'
Barren ridges, gullies, ridges! where the ever-madd'ning flies –
Fiercer than the plagues of Egypt – swarm about your blighted eyes!
Bush! where there is no horizon! where the buried bushman sees
Nothing – Nothing! but the sameness of the ragged, stunted trees!
Lonely hut where drought's eternal, suffocating atmosphere
Where the God-forgotten hatter dreams of city life and beer.

Treacherous tracks that trap the stranger,
endless roads that gleam and glare,
Dark and evil-looking gullies, hiding secrets here and there!
Dull dumb flats and stony rises, where the toiling bullocks bake,
And the sinister 'gohanna', and the lizard, and the snake.
Land of day and night – no morning freshness, and no afternoon,
When the great white sun in rising bringeth summer heat in June.
Dismal country for the exile, when the shades begin to fall
From the sad heart-breaking sunset, to the new-chum worst of all.

Dreary land in rainy weather, with the endless clouds that drift
O'er the bushman like a blanket that the Lord will never lift –
Dismal land when it is raining – growl of floods, and, oh! the woosh
Of the rain and wind together on the dark bed of the bush –
Ghastly fires in lonely humpies where the granite rocks are piled
In the rain-swept wildernesses that are wildest of the wild.

Land where gaunt and haggard women live alone and work like men,
Till their husbands, gone a-droving, will return to them again:
Homes of men! if home had ever such a God-forgotten place,
Where the wild selector's children fly before a stranger's face.
Home of tragedy applauded by the dingoes' dismal yell,
Heaven of the shanty-keeper – fitting fiend for such a hell –
And the wallaroos and wombats, and, of course, the curlew's call –
And the lone sundowner tramping ever onward through it all!

I am back from up the country, up the country where I went
Seeking for the Southern poets' land whereon to pitch my tent;
I have shattered many idols out along the dusty track,
Burnt a lot of fancy verses – and I'm glad that I am back.
I believe the Southern poets' dream will not be realised
Till the plains are irrigated and the land is humanised.
I intend to stay at present, as I said before, in town
Drinking beer and lemon-squashes, taking baths and cooling down.

First published in *The Bulletin*, July 9, 1892

Living in the city vs. living in the Outback – A debate (B)

Please read the following text and collect arguments for a life in the country. Share your ideas with your partner. As a team, try to convince the other group why it is more preferable to live in the outback than to live in the city.

b) A. B. Paterson: In Defense of the Bush

So you're back from up the country, Mister Townsman, where you went,
And you're cursing all the business in a bitter discontent;
Well, we grieve to disappoint you, and it makes us sad to hear
That it wasn't cool and shady – and there wasn't plenty beer,
And the loony bullock snorted when you first came into view;
Well, you know it's not so often that he sees a swell like you;
And the roads were hot and dusty, and the plains were burnt and brown,
And no doubt you're better suited drinking lemon-squash in town.

Yet, perchance, if you should journey down the very track you went
In a month or two at furthest you would wonder what it meant,
Where the sunbaked earth was gasping like a creature in its pain
You would find the grasses waving like a field of summer grain,
And the miles of thirsty gutters blocked with sand and choked with mud,
You would find them mighty rivers with a turbid, sweeping flood;
For the rain and drought and sunshine make no changes in the street,
In the sullen line of buildings and the ceaseless tramp of feet;
But the bush hath moods and changes, as the seasons rise and fall,
And the men who know the bush-land – they are loyal through it all.

But you found the bush was dismal and a land of no delight,
Did you chance to hear a chorus in the shearers' huts at night?
Did they "rise up, William Riley" by the camp-fire's cheery blaze?
Did they rise him as we rose him in the good old droving days?
And the women of the homesteads and the men you chanced to meet –

Were their faces sour and saddened like the "faces in the street",
And the "shy selector children" – were they better now or worse
Than the little city urchins who would greet you with a curse?
Is not such a life much better than the squalid street and square
Where the fallen women flaunt it in the fierce electric glare,
Where the sempstress plies her sewing till her eyes are sore and red
In a filthy, dirty attic toiling on for daily bread?
Did you hear no sweeter voices in the music of the bush
Than the roar of trams and 'buses, and the war-whoop of "the push"?
Did the magpies rouse your slumbers with their carol sweet and strange?
Did you hear the silver chiming of the bell-birds on the range?
But, perchance, the wild birds' music by your senses was despised,
For you say you'll stay in townships till the bush is civilised.
Would you make it a tea-garden and on Sundays have a band
Where the "blokes" might take their "donahs", with a "public" close at hand?
You had better stick to Sydney and make merry with the "push",
For the bush will never suit you, and you'll never suit the bush.

First published in *The Bulletin*, July 9, 1892

Component 3

Aboriginal identities

3.1 Getting started – Speaking about Aboriginal identity

Als Einführung in die beiden Kurzgeschichten *Marlene* (1938) und *Going Home* (1986) ist es sinnvoll, dass sich die Schülerinnen und Schüler zunächst mit dem Hintergrund der australischen Aborigines vertraut machen. Mithilfe dieser Geschichten lernen sie eine weitere Facette in der nationalen Identität Australiens kennen. Die beiden ausgewählten Kurzgeschichten bieten zwei unterschiedliche Perspektiven auf das Leben der australischen Ureinwohner: zum einen werden die sogenannten *Stolen Generations* thematisiert, zum anderen die Schwierigkeit einer gesellschaftlichen Positionierung.
Es gibt schätzungsweise 517.043 *Aborigines* und *Torres Strait Islander* in Australien. Die Torres Strait Islands befinden sich nördlich von Australien und zählen offiziell zu Queensland. Es gibt schätzungsweise 48.000 *Torres Strait Islanders*. Die rechtliche Definition von *Aborigine* und *Torres Strait Islander* ist im Gesetz so fomuliert:

Aboriginal person means a person who
(a) is a member of the Aboriginal race of Australia, and
(b) identifies as an Aboriginal person, and
(c) is accepted by the Aboriginal community as an Aboriginal person.
http://www.legislation.nsw.gov.au/maintop/view/inforce/act+42+1983+cd+0+N [08.12.10]

Torres Strait Islander means a person who
(a) is descended from a Torres Strait Islander, and
(b) identifies as a Torres Strait Islander, and
(c) is accepted as a Torres Strait Islander by a Torres Strait Islander community.
http://www.lawlink.nsw.gov.au/lawlink/childrens_court/c.nsf/pages/CC_aboutusatsiprincipleschildpage [08.12.10]

Diese Definitionen sowie die Grafik und die Bevölkerungszahlen auf ***Copy 16***, die darstellen, in welchen Gebieten und in welchem Zahlenverhältnis die indigene Bevölkerung Australiens lebt, können einem Unterrichtsgespräch vorangestellt werden. Sofern die Schülerinnen und Schüler mit den entsprechenden Themen vertraut sind, können auch Parallelen zu den Ureinwohnern Amerikas sowie zu den Maori in Neuseeland gezogen werden. Die Schülerinnen und Schüler sollen ihre Vorstellung des indigenen Lebens in Australien diskutieren und problematisieren.

Indigenous population distribution in Australia

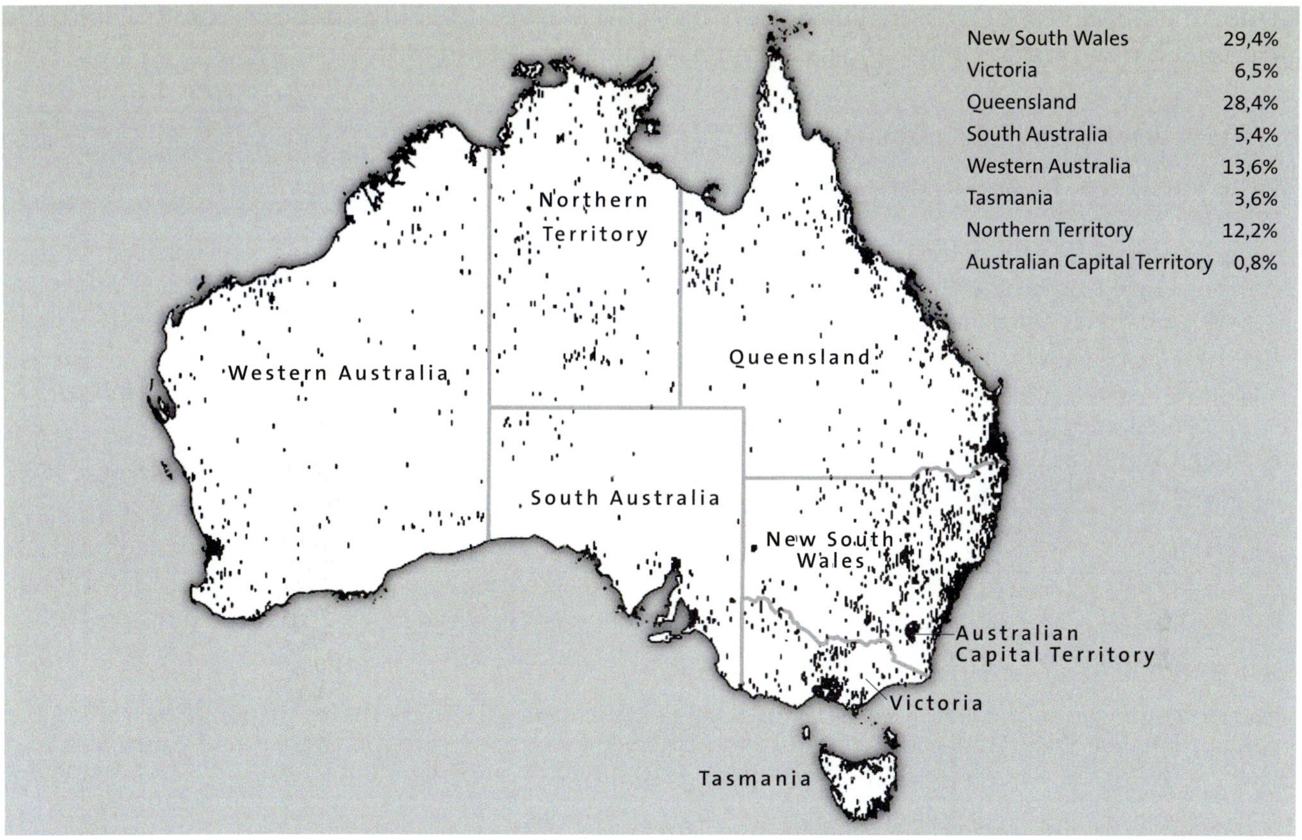

data: Closing the Gap – Prime Minister's Report 2010, www.fahcsia.gov.au/sa/indigenous/pubs/general/Documents/ClosingtheGap2010/sec_1_1.htm [08.12.10]

Pop. Region	Est. non Indigenous pop.	Est. Indigenous pop.
Major Cities of Australia	13,996,450	165,804
Inner Regional Australia	3,975,154	110,643
Outer regional Australia	1,854,026	113,280
Remote Australia	267,199	47,852
Very Remote Australia	88,008	79,464
Total	20,180,837	517,043

data: Social Justice Report 2008, www.hreoc.gov.au/social_justice/sj_report/sjreport08/chap3.html [08.12.10]

Assignments

1. Describe the distribution of indigenous and non-indigenous population in Australia.
2. Which challenges do Aborigines and Torres Strait Islanders face regarding education, jobs, medical care and so on? Take into consideration where the majority of the indigenous population lives.

Definitions of Aboriginal identity

Compare the two very different definitions of Aboriginal identity. Take into consideration that since the colonization of Australia, white people defined Aborigines according to their ancestry.

1) Racist definitions of Aboriginal identity

Caste categories in an identity card used in the 1940s.
From 1910 to the 1940s, white people classified Indigenous people into castes. They defined

- a '**full-blood**' as a person who had no white blood,
- a '**half-caste**' as someone with one white parent,
- a '**quadroon**' or '**quarter-caste**' as someone with an Aboriginal grandfather or grandmother,
- an '**octoroon**' as someone whose great-grandfather or great-grandmother was Aboriginal.

http://www.creativespirits.info/aboriginalculture/people/aboriginal-identity.html [08.12.10]

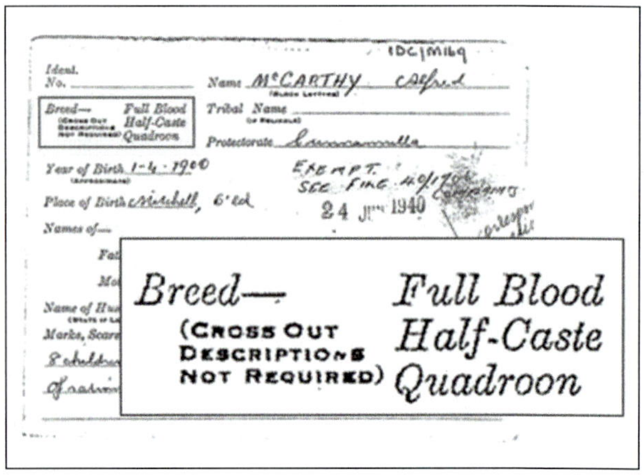
Ident. No.
Name McCARTHY
Tribal Name
Protectorate
Year of Birth
Place of Birth
Names of—
24 JUN 1940
Breed— (Cross Out Descriptions Not Required) Full Blood Half-Caste Quadroon

2) Aboriginal people defining their Aboriginality

Prior to colonization the First People of Australia identified themselves **by their nation**. They would say "I'm a Dharawal man" or "I'm an Eora woman". Some country names around the greater Sydney area include Darug (near Katoomba, Blue Mountains), Gundungurra (near Goulburn, south-west of Sydney), Dharawal (Woolongong), Eora (Sydney). Many Aboriginal people identify themselves as belonging to several nations for example as "Yuwaalaraay and Gamilaraay". This is because

- their **parents or grandparents** come from these nations. Traditionally they would've come from the same nation, but contemporary relationships often involve partners from different Aboriginal nations;
- they have **lived in two places** and identify themselves with each of them.

Another way Aboriginal people identify is **by their boundary or state name**.

Aboriginal boundary (state) names	
State	**Name**
New South Wales	Koori, Goorie, Koorie, Coorie, Murri
Victoria	Koorie
South Australia	Nunga, Nyungar, Nyoongah
Western Australia	Nyungar, Nyoongar
Northern Territory	Yolngu (top end); Anangu (central)
Queensland	Murri
Tasmania	Palawa, Koori

http://www.creativespirits.info/aboriginalculture/people/aboriginal-identity.html [08.12.10]

Assignments

1. Discuss which intention could be behind the first way of classifying the indigenous population.
2. Describe the way the second definition classifies Aboriginal people.

Lösungsvorschläge zu *Copy 16*:

1. The majority of Aboriginal people were killed by the white settlers at the beginning of the colonization of Australia. The number of Aboriginal inhabitants could probably never be restored.

2. Aborigines are always in competition with white Australians. Considering the racism towards the indigenous population, it appears likely that they won't be given the position if they apply for a job together with white Australians. Furthermore, it seems that Aboriginal Australians don't receive a very high level of education, especially in remote places, which is a huge disadvantage in terms of later careers. In cities, Aborigines are most likely to live in the poorer areas and, hence, don't have access to better schools etc. The main reason, however, seems to be that Aborigines are forced into the lifestyle of the white population, which is very different to their own. Since the white population is in the majority, however, Aborigines don't really have a choice.

Lösungsvorschläge zu *Copy 17*:

1. Aborigines and Torres Strait Islanders are mainly in the minority with the exception of remote Australia. One explanation for this might be that the indigenous population might be more adapted to life in the outback. Moreover, life in the cities is expensive so that Aborigines cannot afford this.

2. Mehrere Schülerantworten sind hier möglich, da es um reine Meinungsäußerungen geht. Ein mögliches Tafelbild hierzu könnte wie folgt aussehen:

Education	Jobs	Medical care	Social life
• Institutions of secondary or higher education are hardly available in the outback.	• Due to lack of further education, many jobs aren't available to Aborigines. • Most jobs are only offered in larger cities where life is more expensive.	• Very limited in remote Australia (only provided in emergencies, e.g. Flying Doctors). • Private healthcare not affordable for indigenous population.	• Hardly any social life to be found in the outback (cinemas, theatres, clubs, etc). • Very little social interaction between the indigenous and non-indigenous population.

3.2 Katharine Susannah Prichard: Marlene (1938)

Die Kurzgeschichte *Marlene* setzt sich sowohl mit der Thematik der sogenannten *Stolen Generation* als auch mit dem Schicksal der sogenannten *half-castes* auseinander. Vielen Schülerinnen und Schülern sind beide Thematiken bereits aus den Schuljahren 9 oder 10 bekannt, da sich viele Lehrwerke mit der Geschichte Australiens beschäftigen. Dennoch kann nicht davon ausgegangen werden, dass sich alle Schülerinnen und Schüler ausreichend an diese Unterrichtsreihe erinnern können. Entsprechend ist dieser Unterrichtssequenz zunächst ein Überblick über die Geschichte sowohl der *Stolen Generation* als auch des *National Sorry Day* vorangestellt.

Im Mittelpunkt dieser ersten Stunde steht entsprechend die historische Perspektive, ohne die ein Verstehen der Kurzgeschichte nur schwer möglich wäre. Die Schülerinnen und Schüler sollen erkennen, dass die *Stolen Generation* auch heute noch von großer Bedeutung und politischer Brisanz für das Verhältnis zwischen der weißen und der indigenen Bevölkerung Australiens ist. Für den Gegenwartsbezug sorgt entsprechend die Rede des Premierminister Australiens, Kevin Rudd, die in Partnerarbeit oder als Hausaufgabe als Vorübung für eine Klausur analysiert werden könnte.
Die ersten beiden Texte können als Einstieg genutzt werden und nach gemeinsamen Lesen mit der gesamten Gruppe diskutiert werden. ***Copy 18*** dient hierbei zur generellen Information bzw. Auffrischung des Hintergrundwissens.
Die Beantwortung der Frage auf ***Copy 19*** sieht allein die eigene Meinungsäußerung der Schülerinnen und Schüler vor. Sollten diese jedoch einen Denkanstoß brauchen, kann die Lehrperson Impulse zum Pro und Kontra des *National Sorry Day* geben, wie z. B.:

- Consider how survivors of the *Stolen Generation* feel: they have lost their families and their sense of belonging and they were never able to live a life that their families might have wished for them. Can they really forgive?
- Do actions speak louder than words? Would financial compensation be more helpful than a mere apology? Or is it impossible to value their loss in money anyway and, is a symbolic gesture, therefore, more helpful?
- Draw a comparison to the Maori in New Zealand and the Native Americans in the USA or Canada. Research on the actions these governments have taken in order to apologize for their deeds.

Das Internet bietet eine reichhaltige Informationsquelle bezüglich der *Stolen Generation*, so können sich die Schülerinnen und Schüler im Rahmen einer Vertiefung entweder in Gruppen oder individuell als Hausaufgabe näher über die Thematik informieren.
Mögliche Webseiten wären:

- www.eniar.org/stolengenerations.html
- www.nla.gov.au/digicoll/bringing-them-home-online.html
- www.aiatsis.gov.au/

Die Konzeption dieses Unterrichtsmodells setzt voraus, dass die Kurzgeschichte als vorbereitende Lektüre gelesen wird.

The Stolen Generation

"When they take our land, they take the ground of our culture.
When they take our children, they take the future of our culture.
If they keep on taking, there will be nothing left."[1]

The Stolen Generations

Between 1910 and 1970, up to 100,000 Aboriginal children were taken forcibly or under duress from their families by police or welfare officers.
Most were under 5 years old. There was rarely any judicial process. To be Aboriginal was enough. They are known as the 'Stolen Generations'.

What happened to them?

- Most were raised in Church or state institutions. Some were fostered or adopted by white parents.
- Many suffered physical and sexual abuse. Food and living conditions were poor.
- They received little education, and were expected to go into low-grade domestic and farming work.

Why were they taken?

They were taken because it was Federal and State Government policy that Aboriginal children – especially those of mixed Aboriginal and European descent – should be removed from their parents.
Between 10 and 30% of all Aboriginal children were removed and in some places, these policies continued into the 1970s.

- The main motive was to 'assimilate' Aboriginal children into European society over one or two generations by denying and destroying their Aboriginality.
- Speaking their languages and practising their ceremonies was forbidden.
- They were taken miles from their country, some overseas.
- Parents were not told where their children were and could not trace them.
- Children were told they were orphans.
- Family visits were discouraged or forbidden; letters were destroyed.

What were the results?

The physical and emotional damage to those taken away was profound and lasting:

- Most grew up in a hostile environment without family ties or cultural identity.
- As adults, many suffered insecurity, lack of self esteem, feelings of worthlessness, depression, suicide, violence, delinquency, abuse of alcohol and drugs and inability to trust.
- Lacking a parental model, many had difficulty bringing up their own children.

The scale of separation also had profound consequences for the whole Aboriginal community – anger, powerlessness and lack of purpose as well as an abiding distrust of Government, police and officials.

http://www.eniar.org/stolengenerations.html [09.12.10]

[1] from: *An Indigenous Home for Indigenous Children* – speech by Michael Dodson, Aboriginal and Torres Strait Islander Social Justice Commissioner at the SNAICC National Conference, Townsville, June 1997.

History of Sorry Day

On 26th May 1997 the Report of the National Inquiry into the Separation of Aboriginal and Torres Strait Islander children from their families was tabled in Federal Parliament. The Bringing Them Home Report, revealed the extent of forced removal policies, which went on for 150 years into the early 1980s. The Report revealed the devastating effects of these policies in terms of spiritual, emotional and physical trauma, as a direct result from the broken connection to traditional land, culture and language, the separation of families and the effect of these on parenting skills. It also revealed the trans-generational impact and damaging effects that these forced child removals continue to have on the Indigenous families and communities today.

The release of the findings of the BTH Report had a profound effect on the Australian public. The Report detailed unquestionable evidence about the forced removal of thousands of Indigenous children from their families and communities. The most shocking finding of the report was that to date, not one Aboriginal family had escaped the effects of the forced removal policies. When the knowledge of these policies became public the National Sorry Day Committee united the Australian public in a grass roots movement that shifted the Nation.

The first Sorry Day was held in Sydney in 1998, it is now commemorated nationally with thousands of Australians from all walks of life participating in memorial services, commemorative meetings, survival celebrations and community gatherings to honour the Stolen Generations.

Sorry Day has helped to keep a focus and the issue of the Stolen Generations on both the political and social agenda with the ensuing results including:

- The Bringing Them Home Report selling more copies than any comparable report.
- Hundreds and Thousands of non-Indigenous Australians have signed Sorry Books.
- Many thousands of Australians have attended Sorry Day commemorative events.
- Over one and half million Australians walked bridges in support of the Stolen Generations and Reconciliation.
- On Wednesday 13th February the Prime Minister Rudd and the Australian Parliament said "SORRY" to the Stolen Generations, their families and communities.

http://www.nsdc.org.au/home/index.php?option=com_content&view=category&layout=blog&id=20&Itemid=51 [08.12.10]

Assignment

Do you think that a National Sorry Day might help to improve the relationship between the indigenous and non-indigenous population?

Kevin Rudd: Speech (2008)

Kevin Rudd was the Australian Prime Minister from 3 December 2007 until 24 June 2010.

Today we honour the Indigenous peoples of this land, the oldest continuing cultures in human history. We reflect on their past mistreatment. We reflect in particular on the mistreatment of those who were Stolen Generations – this blemished chapter in our nation's history. The time has now come for the nation to turn a new page in Australia's history by righting the wrongs of the past and so moving forward with confidence to the future. We apologise for the laws and policies of successive Parliaments and governments that have inflicted profound grief, suffering and loss on these our fellow Australians. We apologise especially for the removal of Aboriginal and Torres Strait Islander children from their families, their communities and their country.

For the pain, suffering and hurt of these Stolen Generations, their descendants and for their families left behind, we say sorry.

To the mothers and the fathers, the brothers and the sisters, for the breaking up of families and communities, we say sorry.

And for the indignity and degradation thus inflicted on a proud people and a proud culture, we say sorry.

We the Parliament of Australia respectfully request that this apology be received in the spirit in which it is offered as part of the healing of the nation.

For the future we take heart; resolving that this new page in the history of our great continent can now be written.

We today take this first step by acknowledging the past and laying claim to a future that embraces all Australians.

A future where this Parliament resolves that the injustices of the past must never, never happen again.

A future where we harness the determination of all Australians, Indigenous and non-Indigenous, to close the gap that lies between us in life expectancy, educational achievement and economic opportunity.

A future where we embrace the possibility of new solutions to enduring problems where old approaches have failed.

A future based on mutual respect, mutual resolve and mutual responsibility.

A future where all Australians, whatever their origins, are truly equal partners, with equal opportunities and with an equal stake in shaping the next chapter in the history of this great country, Australia.

http://www.news.com.au/apology-to-the-stolen-generations/story-e6frfkp9–1111115539655 [09.12.10]

Assignments

1. Briefly summarize the speech.
2. Which rhetorical devices does Kevin Rudd employ in order to appear genuine as well as to convince listeners of the importance of this apology?
3. Do you consider this speech helpful in the process of reconciliation?

Lösungsvorschlag zu *Copy 19*:
Mehrere Schülerantworten sind hier möglich, da es um reine Meinungsäußerungen geht.

Lösungsvorschlag zu *Copy 20*:

1. In his speech from 2008, the Australian Prime Minister Kevin Rudd apologizes on behalf of the Australian government to the Aborigines for all the harm that has been done to them. He apologizes especially to those who belong to the so-called Stolen Generation and asks for the Aborigines to accept this apology. Furthermore, he emphasizes that in future all Australians should respect each other.
2. Schüler könnten folgende rhetorische Mittel benennen:
   - Use of personal pronoun "we" to include all non-indigenous Australians, as well as involve all listeners.
   - Metaphor ("to turn the page in Australia's history", l. 4): demonstrating moving on from all past horrors can be easy.
   - Parallelism (ll. 6–10): emphasizes Rudd's message.
   - Anaphora ("A future", ll. 22–30): see parallelism.
   - Use of rather simple language and short sentences: the speaker makes it possible for everyone to understand his message, which is directed to the whole of Australia's population.
3. Individuelle Schülerantworten sind hier möglich, da es um Meinungsäußerungen geht.

3.3 The "half-castes"

Die *Stolen Generation* umfasst, wie schon zuvor erwähnt, nicht nur Aborigines, sondern auch Menschen, deren Eltern oder Großeltern sowohl Aborigines als auch weiße Siedler waren. Es ist wichtig, auf den hier verwendeten Begriff der *half-castes* hinzuweisen und diesen zu problematisieren, da er aus der rassistischen Theoretisierung von Seiten der Weißen in Australien stammt. In dieser Kurzgeschichte ist der Handlungsort ein Camp für sogenannte *half-castes*, in dem die Figuren unter menschenunwürdigen Bedingungen leben. Albert, einer der Campbewohner, äußert sich zu der schwierigen Situation, in der sich diese Menschen befinden (S. 52–54). Dieser Textausschnitt kann als Einstieg in die Textarbeit genutzt werden. Hierbei werden die Schülerinnen und Schüler aufgefordert, den entsprechenden Abschnitt aus der Fragestellung, ob die Campbewohner nun als schwarz oder weiß gelten bzw. wie sie sich selbst sehen, zu analysieren.
Fragestellung und Ergebnissammlung an der Tafel könnten entsprechend wie folgt aussehen:

Read the abstract and analyse it according to whether the characters are viewed as black or white and how they perceive themselves.

Question of identity

Not black	Not white
• Belong: can live with black people as long as they have no contact at all with whites. • Do not belong: because of contact with whites, they can read & write, have different views on hygiene and aspire to a different lifestyle. ↓ *"Westernized"* *Not considered black*	• Educated as Christians, taken away from their Aboriginal families and grow up separately. • Have no rights. • Aren't allowed to inherit. • Live in camps and work as servants. • Aren't allowed to get married and have children etc. ↓ *Not considered human*

Die Kurzgeschichte bietet sich für genauere Charakteranalysen bzw. Gegenüberstellungen an. Es ist wiederum Albert, der pointiert eine *half-caste*, Mrs Jackson, mit einer Weißen, Mrs Boyd, vergleicht. Der Textausschnitt (S. 52–54) eignet sich für eine solche Gegenüberstellung, die noch einmal die grausame Ungerechtigkeit darstellt. Er kann ebenfalls für eine Überleitung in die nächste, zeitintensivere Aufgabenstellung genutzt werden. Die Ergebnissicherung findet auch als Tafelbild statt:

Work with your partner and compare the two characters.

Comparison of two characters

Mrs Boyd	Mrs Jackson
• Granddaughter of early settler who killed many Aboriginal people • Land and law	• Granddaughter of one of the few survivors • Related to best families

3.4 A role play

Bei der näheren Analyse der Charaktere in dieser Kurzgeschichte ist die Vier-Ecken-Methode hilfreich. Da es möglich ist, sich hier auf vier Charaktere zu konzentrieren, wird jeder Ecke des Kursraumes ein Charakter zugeordnet; so kann sich jede Schülerin und jeder Schüler eine Figur auswählen und entsprechend in diese Ecke gehen. Zunächst sollen die vier Gruppen klären, aus welchen Gründen sie sich für diese Figur interessieren. Danach wird ein Sprecher pro Gruppe bestimmt, der diese Figur in einem anschließenden Rollenspiel darstellen soll. Die Arbeit verläuft anhand der Beantwortung der Fragen auf den *role cards*.

Role card 1: *Mrs Boyd*

- Familiarize yourselves with Mrs Boyd's situation: where does she live/come from? Why has she come to speak to the Aborigines?
- What is Mrs Boyd's interest in Mollie?
- She has to ask for Marlene six times, but does not receive an answer. How does she explain this and how would she feel about this?

Role card 2: *Miss Cecily Allison*

- Miss Allison is an outsider to the situation, as she comes from England. Describe her motives for accompanying Mrs Boyd.
- Is she influenced by Mrs Boyd's perspective or does she have her own, possibly different, opinion?
- How would she speak to the Aborigines if she came back on her own?

Role card 3: *Albert*

- Albert appears to be quite rude and is told off for this. Do you consider his behaviour as rude? How do you explain his rudeness?
- What do you learn about his life story?

Role card 4: *Mollie*

- Try to imagine yourselves in Mollie's position. What could be the reasons for her naivety about men? Do you think she was aware of the risks of getting pregnant?
- Does she know what might happen to her baby if the whites are aware of its existence?

Nach der Erarbeitungsphase bekommt die Gruppe die Möglichkeit, den jeweiligen Sprecher auf seine Rolle vorzubereiten. Die vier Sprecher setzen sich nun zu dem Lehrer in die Mitte des Raumes, der Rest der Lerngruppe positioniert sich um diesen Kreis. Der Lehrer wird nun das Rollenspiel leiten, indem er unterschiedliche Fragen an die unterschiedlichen Figuren stellt, die dann direkt zueinander sprechen können. In dieser Identifikation mit den jeweiligen Figuren ist es wichtig, dass die Lehrkraft in den Hintergrund tritt und nur eingreift, wenn einige zu wenig/zu viel zu dem Gespräch beitragen.
Mögliche Fragen könnten wie folgt lauten:

- **Albert**, please tell Miss Alison how do you feel about her coming to visit the camp and wanting to write about this. Do you think this might help your situation?
- **Mollie**, explain to Mrs Boyd why you risked having a baby when you know that you aren't allowed to have a family and that Marlene might be taken away from you?
- **Mrs Boyd**, how do you feel about being compared to Mrs Jackson by Albert? Does it make you doubt your right to rule over these people?
- **Miss Alison**, please explain to Mollie and Albert the motivation behind writing your book?
- **Mrs Boyd**, tell Miss Alison what you think about her way of communicating with the people in the camp.
- **Albert**, please advise Mollie on which steps to take next.

- **Mollie**, please share with Albert how you felt when the people in the camp were trying to hide you.
- **Miss Alison** please tell Mrs Boyd how you feel about the way she treats the people in the camp.

Lösungsansätze:

Mrs Boyd:

- Quotation: "A good horsewoman, capable of managing her own affairs […]. Her manner was authoritative, but kind and friendly."
- Interpretation: She is portrayed as a woman of power, who is used to ruler over others.
  Quotation: "the ugliest scrap of humanity she had ever seen, but there was something familiar in its tiny crumpled face."
- Interpretation: Clearly shows that she does not value the people in the camp as human beings. Allows the interpretation that she may possibly know the white father of the child.
- Quotation: "They're an immoral lot, these half-castes."
  Interpretation: Displays that she does not even think about the inhumane situation the people in the camp have to bear, but judges them on moral grounds.

Mollie:

- Quotation: "I been going with two or three boys in town."
  1st possible interpretation: indicates that Mollie has no self-respect. For her it appears to be normal to be involved with more men.
  2nd possible interpretation which is indicated by the group's reaction to Mollie's statement: "a sigh, as of relief, and a titter of suppressed mirth escaped" – the father is not to be named and is possibly close to Mrs Boyd, which is emphasized by Mrs Boyd's own statement.
  Quotation: "Don't be angry […] I couldn't help it … and I like the baby."
  Interpretation: shows that she respects Mrs Boyd, but she really wanted to have this baby and care for it. It's also possible that she does not know about contraception.

Miss Cecily Allison:

- Quotation: "Do the aboriginals treat half-castes better?"
  Interpretation: shows consideration for the people and indicates that she does not view them as fairly treated by the white people.
- Quotation: "But what about the whites who are responsible for them?"
  Interpretation: illustrates that she is concerned about the lack of responsibility the whites feel for the indigenous people who work for them.

Albert:

- Quotation: "It's a hell of a place to see."
  Interpretation: he may mean this literally, as this camp appears to be hell on earth for the people who are forced to live there.

- Quotation: "All the land about has been taken up." etc./"My own people!" etc.
  Interpretation: Albert sees the situation clearly and isn't afraid to openly criticize both the unfair treatment in general as well as Mrs Boyd in particular, although he is threatened by her for doing so.

3.5 Analysing Archie Weller's *Going Home* (1986)

Die Kurzgeschichte von Archie Weller setzt sich mit der gegenwärtigen Schwierigkeit einer gesellschaftlichen Positionierung der Aborigines auseinander sowie mit den Fragen nach deren Bildung und sozialem Status.
Zu Beginn der Auseinandersetzung mit dieser *short story* und ihrer Thematik bietet es sich zunächst an, den Protagonisten William Jacob Woodward genauer zu analysieren, um sich davon ausgehend mit der Situation der Aborigines auseinanderzusetzen. Dies geschieht nach der *STEAL*-Methode (s. ***Copy 21***).

Nachdem sich die Schülerinnen und Schüler nun mit der Hauptfigur vertraut gemacht haben, können sie herausstellen, wie sehr sich Billy Woodward von anderen Aborigines unterscheidet. Die folgende Arbeit nach dem *Jigsaw*-Prinzip (s. ***Copy 22***) macht die Schülerinnen und Schüler mit dem statistisch erfassten realen Leben der indigenen Bevölkerung Australiens vertraut. Hier spielen nun auch die anderen männlichen Familienmitglieder eine Rolle, die keiner genaueren Charakterisierung bedürfen, da sie nur Nebencharaktere sind und hier nur zur Veranschaulichung des Sachverhaltes dienen.
Um diesen Themenbereich abzurunden, soll der Verlauf von Billys Leben von seiner Schulzeit bis zu seiner Verhaftung noch einmal dargestellt werden. Hierbei können sich die Schülerinnen und Schüler in Kleingruppen einen Verlauf erarbeiten, der anhand der Folie im Plenum überprüft werden kann.

Zum Abschluss dieses Components ist ein Rückblick auf *Component 1* zu empfehlen, da sich ein Vergleich zwischen den Anfängen Australien als Strafkolonie für Weiße und dem heutigen Australien anbietet, in dem vor allem die indigene Bevölkerung Verbrechen zu begehen scheint. Somit ist ein direkter Vergleich zwischen zwei Identitäten Australiens möglich.
Die Schülerinnen und Schüler werden zunächst mit der *STEAL*-Methode vertraut gemacht, die helfen soll, eine indirekte Charakterisierung zu erstellen (zur Charakterisierung vgl. auch *Component 2*). Dabei kann zunächst die Methode selbst in einem Lehrervortrag erklärt werden.
In dem bereits erklärten *Think-Pair-Share*-Verfahren setzen sich die einzelnen Schülerinnen und Schüler zunächst individuell mit der Tabelle auseinander und suchen nach Belegen im Text. Dann tauschen sie sich mit ihrem Partner aus, bevor alle Ergebnisse im Plenum diskutiert werden.

3.6 Background information: Aboriginal Australia

Um die heutige Situation der Aborigines besser beurteilen zu können, werden die Schülerinnen und Schüler im nächsten Schritt besser mit den Lebensumständen der Aborigines vertraut gemacht. In Form eines *expert group jigsaws* werden drei unterschiedliche Aspekte erarbeitet, um die Analyse des vorliegenden Materials zu optimieren. Die Informationen werden in drei entsprechenden Expertengruppen erarbeitet und dann in der sogenannten Heimatgruppe ausgetauscht.
In den einzelnen Gruppen soll diskutiert werden, inwiefern sowohl die Hauptfigur als auch seine männlichen Familienmitglieder einem realistischen und statistisch erfassten indigenen Australier entsprechen. Dabei soll vor allem auf die Faktoren geachtet werden, die den Bildungschancen von Aborigines im Wege stehen, bzw. welche Faktoren für die hohen Verbrechensraten verantwortlich sind.
Im Plenum kann nun diskutiert werden, wie die Schüler und Schülerinnen das Leben der indigenen Bevölkerung Australiens einschätzen. Je nach Zeitrahmen lassen sich Parallelen zu den *Native Americans* ziehen.

3.7 The rise and fall of William Jacob Woodward

Zum Abschluss dieses Components soll noch einmal auf die Hauptfigur eingegangen werden. Hierzu kann ***Copy 25*** auf Folie kopiert und am OHP schrittweise mit den Schülerinnen und Schülern erarbeitet werden.

Writing an indirect characterization

Speech	What does the character say? How does the character speak?
Thought	What is revealed through the character's private thoughts and feelings?
Effect on others toward the character	What is revealed through the character's effect on others? How do other characters feel or behave in reaction to the character?
Actions	What does the character do? How does the character behave?
Looks	What does the character look like? How does the character dress?

	Character:	
	Your own description:	**Quotation:**
Speech		
Thought		
Effect on others toward the character		
Actions		
Looks		

Lösungsvorschlag zu *Copy 21*:

	Character: William Jacob Woodward	
	Your own description:	**Quotation:**
Speech	• Elaborate, educated, avoids colloquial expressions (especially noticeable in comparison to the other characters)	• "Certainly. Help yourself." • "I wasn't causing any trouble, and I wasn't in any robbery. I like the way you come straight down here when there's trouble."
Thought	• Change from the time before and after the arrest: self-confident, wanting to return home, then scared and helpless	• "he can walk the earth with pride, as his ancestors did many years before him." • arrest: "suddenly feels small and naked."
Effect on others toward the character	• Estranged from his ancestry/family • Good relationship with his brother and cousin	• "he never saw his people: his dark, silent staring people, his rowdy, brawling, drunk people." • relationship to his mother: "feels unsure and alone."
Actions	• University graduate • Successful painter • Modern, contemporary • Behaves like a non-Aboriginal person • At first very self-confident • Scared and insecure at the time of the arrest	• "Now, on his twenty-first birthday" • "had his first exhibition of paintings a month ago. They sold well […]" • "for five years he has worked hard and saved and sacrificed." • "new car, new clothes, new life" • "*He* was white now." • "returns his gaze with the look of a cornered dingo who does not understand how he was trapped."
Looks	• Aborigine	• "his movements are elegant and delicate. His hair is well-groomed, and his clothes are clean." • "when it comes down to it all, he is just a black man."

Aboriginal Australia – An expert group jigsaw

Expert group 1: The average Aboriginal Australian's life

Read the information below. Compare these figures with
a) with William Jacob Woodward and
b) his brother, cousin and father.

In how far does the text give a realistic image of the average Aboriginal Australian?

Birth	The Aboriginal newborn joins 2.3 per cent of the Australian **population**. Their family consists of 3.5 people, compared to a non-Indigenous **family** which averages about 2.6 people. Chances are at 12.6% that the newborn will be of low birth weight, double the rate of non-Indigenous babies. Low birth weight determines many health factors later in life. [...]
18 years old	The average Indigenous Australian has dropped out of **school** last year. [...] Now that they're over 15, they are likely to be obese or **overweight** – 61% more likely, compared to non-Indigenous Australians (48 percent).
20 years old	20 years was the **median age** for the entire Indigenous population in 2001, while on average the non-Indigenous population was 36 years old. They probably move into a metropolitan or **urban area**, as do 75% of their peers. The average Indigenous Australian has trouble **finding work**. They are likely to join 27% of their age group who are unemployed. [...]
25 years old	About six per cent of the average Aboriginal Australian's Indigenous compatriots will be in **prison**. [...] On average, it is very likely that some member of an average Aboriginal Australian's family is in prison right now. In about two year's time **their father dies**. [...] They can only dream of going to **university**. Less than 2% of the Aboriginal population goes to university compared to more than 4% of the non-Indigenous population who do. As a male, 108 of his peer group of 100,000 would have committed **suicide** by now, 40% more than in the general population.
30 years old	The average Indigenous Australian has already **lived half of their life**. [...]
50 years old	If they lived in a remote area, the average Australian Aboriginal person **dies** before they reach the age of 50, 35 years before their non-Indigenous countrymen would die. [...]
60 years old	An average Australian Aboriginal person **dies** (if they lived in a city) while his non-Indigenous peer lives for another 24 years.

data: http://www.creativespirits.info/aboriginalculture/people/aboriginal-statistic-timeline.html [09.12.10] (adapted)

Expert group 2: Aboriginal education

Read the information below. Compare these figures with
c) William Jacob Woodward and
d) his brother, cousin and father.

In how far does the text give a realistic image of the average Aboriginal Australian?

60%	Percentage of Aboriginal children significantly behind non-Aboriginal children by the time they start Year One.
40%	Percentage by which an Aboriginal student's chance of employment rises if they complete year 10 or 11. Completing Year 12 increases employment prospects by a further 13%.
3%	Percentage of Aboriginal students who complete a university degree.
20,000	Number of Aboriginal university graduates in Australia in 2006. In 1991 this figure was at 3,600.
36%	Percentage of people in remote communities with access to a library.
24%	Percentage of people in remote communities with a school that only goes up to year 12. 29% have a school up to year 10.
10%	Percentage of Aboriginal children who graduate from year 12.
40%	Percentage of Aboriginal children who stay at school until year 12, compared to 76% among non-Indigenous children.
21%	Percentage of Indigenous people aged 15–64 who had completed year 12 in 2008. Same figure in 2002: 18%; figure for non-Indigenous people in 2008: 54%.
46.5%	Retention rate of Indigenous students in 2008. Same figure in 1995: 30.7%.

data: http://www.creativespirits.info/aboriginalculture/education/index.html [09.12.10] (adapted)

What impedes Aboriginal education?

Factors which hamper Aboriginal students' education are

- **English teaching materials**, because many Aboriginal students' first language is not English.
- **Inappropriate context:** if the stories told in teaching materials do not relate to Indigenous lives, they are of little use for Aboriginal students.
- **No ‚black faces':** if teaching material (books, films) is entirely based on white models, Indigenous students cannot identify with their characters.
- **Poverty:** because parents cannot afford health services, students have poorer health than their peers. Hearing loss is one consequence with all its side effects which affect learning.
- **Lack of infrastructure:** analysis showed that for every dollar spent by the government on the education of a child in the Northern Territory, just 47 cents was spent educating a child in a remote community (Wadeye). And if all children of that community attended school, there wouldn't be enough teachers and classrooms to accommodate them all […].
- **Connection to their communities:** many Aboriginal people like to reside in their own communities and will not leave them for skills training.
- **Uneducated parents:** Native Welfare took Aboriginal children away up until the late 1970s. Aboriginal parents where one parent was white were in constant fear that if they sent their children to school they would never see them again. "I went to school late, I think, because the old people were concerned about Native Welfare taking half caste kids away. They were hiding me in the bloody scrub, until they stopped taking these kids away," says Trevor Parker, a Punjima Aboriginal man from the Pilbara region in Western Australia […].

http://www.creativespirits.info/aboriginalculture/education/index.html#ixzz10GNmzBK9 [09.12.10] (adapted)

Expert group 3: Aboriginal law and justice statistics

Read the information below. Compare these figures with
e) William Jacob Woodward and
f) his brother, cousin and father.

In how far does the text give a realistic image of the average Aboriginal Australian?

83 %	Percentage of the prison population in the Northern Territory which is Indigenous.
24 %	Percentage of the prison population in Australia which is Indigenous [14]. Aboriginal people make up 2.5 % of the Australian population.
14	Times an Aboriginal person is more likely to be locked up than non-Indigenous Australians.
58 %	Percentage of juveniles detained in Australia who are Indigenous [18]. Same figure for NSW: 56 %. Percentage of NSW population: 4.4 %.
70 %	Percentage of youth in prison that have been sexually assaulted as children.
48 %	Percentage by which the Indigenous imprisonment rate of NSW rose between 2001 and 2008.
$269	Daily cost to the Australian government to keep a prisoner locked up.
$271	Daily rate for an Executive Room at the Hilton in Sydney, including breakfast buffet.
$1b	Money the NSW government spends each year to maintain its prison system.
11	Times an Aboriginal child aged between 10 and 14 is likely to be charged by the police.
28	Times an Indigenous male child is more likely to be placed in juvenile detention [11]. The rate for female children is 24 times.
3.6	Average sentence length of Indigenous prisoners in years (non-Indigenous: 5.3).
48 %	Percentage of Aboriginal juveniles who end up in court. Same figure for non-Indigenous juveniles: 28 %.

data: http://www.creativespirits.info/aboriginalculture/law/index.html [09.12.10] (adapted)

Aboriginal prison rates

As an Indigenous adult you are 14 times more likely to be incarcerated. Juveniles in Western Australia are 48 times more likely to be imprisoned than their white peers
Half of the 10 to 17-year-olds in jails are Indigenous

Where do these prison rates come from?

To understand these high rates, one must know Aboriginal history. Many factors work together and some of them include the following:

- **Stolen Generations.** Those taken away from their families as a child are twice as likely to be arrested as their peers.
- **Police behaviour.** Police might act in a racist, violent or inappropriate manner (see below for more on this).
- **Offence criminalization.** Aboriginal people are 15 times more likely to be charged for swearing or offensive behaviour than the rest of the community.
- **Social and economic situation.** Poverty and unemployment, particularly in the case of young Aboriginal people or in rural and remote areas.
- **People's attitude.** Some police and community members have a „law and order" attitude.
- **Lack of language skills.** Some Aboriginal people are sentenced to jail without them fully understanding the court process because English is not their first language.
- **Foetal alcohol syndrome.** Many children enter the justice system because their mother drank too much alcohol during her pregnancy. Her children are often unable to appreciate the consequences of their actions.
- **Family breakdown** due to various social factors.

http://www.creativespirits.info/aboriginalculture/law/aboriginal-prison-rates.html [09.12.10] (adapted)

The rise and fall of William Jacob Woodward

At the age of 16 (last year at school):

- "Last year at school"
- spends a lot of time with his brother and cousin
- "Schoolwork, and learning, and discipline"
- "No one can stop him now. He forgets about the river of his Dreaming and the people of his blood and the girl in his heart."

At the age of 18:

- "picked by a top city team as a rover"
- "played for the state"
- "never went out to the park at Guildford, so he never saw his people"
- "*was* white now"
- sees one of his uncles, "shouted at the old man and pushed him down the steps"

End of 5th year (approx. 20 years old):

- "All the teachers were proud of him."
- "went to the Australian Institute of Technology to further his painting"
- "cut off his long hair"
- "tall and proud, with sensitive lips of a dreamer"
- "went to nightclubs"
- sees one of his aunts, "felt ashamed to be related to a thing like that. He was bitter that she was of his blood"

Turning point:

- Last match, "young part-Aboriginal opponent who stared at him the whole game", "boy's family picked him up", Billy sees "the children kicking an old football about with yells and shouts of laughter."
- "So Billy was going home, because he had been reminded of home (with all its carefree joys)."

- Returns home, gets unfairly arrested along with his brother and his cousin; neither his prior successes nor his education can save him from the arrest, as they do not matter back home.

Component 4

Multicultural identity

4.1 Getting started – Speaking about migrant identity

Tom Winton: Neighbours (1985)

Zum Einstieg in die Thematik sollen die Schülerinnen und Schüler mithilfe von ***Copy 24*** Informationen über multikulturelle Identitäten in ihrem eigenen Klassenraum zusammentragen. In einem zweiten Schritt sollen sich die Schülerinnen und Schüler dann nach dem *Think-Pair-Share*-Verfahren individuell und in Stillarbeit Gedanken über den Titel der *short story* machen, ohne diese zunächst mit dem Partner zu teilen. Anschließend tauschen sich die Partner miteinander aus.

Think about the title of the short story and then share your ideas with your partner.

Nach wenigen Minuten erfolgt ein generelles Feedback. Es sollte möglichst erreicht werden, dass Schlüsselbegriffe wie „community" oder „conflict" genannt werden.
In Partnerarbeit beschäftigen sich die Schülerinnen und Schüler nun zur Einstimmung mit dem ersten Abschnitt der Erzählung. Sie sollen darauf achten, wie die unterschiedlichen Nachbarn, nicht jedoch das dargestellte Ehepaar, zunächst dargestellt werden. Diese Übung soll dazu beitragen, dass die Lernenden die Perspektive des jungen Ehepaares einnehmen, um das Verständnis für dieses zu ermöglichen.

Work with your partner and find out how the neighbours are presented in the first paragraph (p. 82).

Ein Tafelbild könnte die folgende Form haben:

Macedonian family	Polish widower
• "The Macedonian family shouted, ranted, screamed. It took months for the newcomers to comprehend the fact that their neighbours were not murdering each other, merely talking."	• "spend most of his day hammering nails into wood only to pull them out again" • "yard was stacked with salvaged lumber. He added to it, but did not build with it."

Im Anschluss an diesen Einstieg sollen sich die Schülerinnen und Schüler nun mit den folgenden Fragen auseinandersetzen. Hierbei arbeiten die Lernenden in Vierergruppen, in denen jeweils ein Sprecher bestimmt wird, in Anlehnung an das Prinzip des Team Interviews, indem zunächst A mit B und C mit D die Fragen beantwortet. Anschließend tauschen sich alle vier gemeinsam über ihre Ergebnisse aus. Somit können nicht nur Ideen ausgetauscht werden, es lassen sich auch alternative Ansichten austauschen. Das Feedback am Ende dieser Übung erfolgt durch die jeweiligen bestimmten Sprecher aus jeder Vierergruppe.

1. Do they seem like neighbours you would like to have?
2. Which type of characterization is this and whose perspective could this be written in?
3. Which conclusion can be drawn from this observation about the young couple's attitude towards their neighbours?

Mögliche Antworten könnten folgendermaßen ausfallen:

1. Meinungsäußerung (z. B. perfect neighbours, impossible to live with such neighbours, etc.).
2. This is a direct characterization written in the perspective of the young couple. It reflects their neglect of the neighbours' cultural background.
3. The young couple doesn't feel comfortable around their neighbours, as they seem messy, chaotic, loud and not well adapted to Australian society.

Die Schülerinnen und Schüler haben sich nun ein Bild über die Figuren gemacht und sollten möglichst zu dem Ergebnis kommen, dass die Erzählhaltung die Perspektive des jungen Ehepaares ist, obwohl sie noch relativ oberflächlich und im Wesentlichen nicht personalisiert ist.

Die dritte Frage ermöglicht nun den Übergang zum Lesen der gesamten Kurzgeschichte, da die Voreingenommenheit des jungen Ehepaares gegenüber ihrer Nachbarn deutlich geworden ist. Der Fokus sollte hierbei auf den Vorurteilen liegen, die alle Figuren zu haben scheinen. Hierbei können die Schülerinnen und Schüler in ihren Gruppen ***Copy 25*** vervollständigen.

Your multicultural classroom

You will need to **walk and talk** during this activity. Try to find a different person for each of the questions below. Do not forget you can include your teacher as well!

Find someone who ...	Name
has travelled to another continent outside Europe.	
has lived in another country.	
speaks another language at home.	
can say "Hello" in Arabic.	
knows one Yiddish word.	
does sports invented in Asia.	
was born outside Germany.	
has a citizenship other than German.	
is related to someone living in Poland.	
can count to 5 in Japanese/Russian/French or any other language (except English and German).	
can name one country next to Turkey.	
has friends outside Germany.	
has partaken in Ramadan.	
knows how to dance the Tango.	
knows three different types of pasta.	
has eaten at a Japanese restaurant.	
knows what "Vla" is.	

Prejudices

In your group, work out the prejudices the characters have about each other. Find quotations that solely indicate the characters' opinions; also state what the prejudices show you about the characters themselves. Who appears to be the most prejudiced and who does not judge the others?

	Macedonian family	Young couple	Polish widower
Quotation:			
Interpretation:			

Lösungsvorschlag zu *Copy 25*:

	Macedonian family	Young couple	Polish widower
Quotation:	"raised eyebrows at the late hour at which the newcomers rose in the mornings" "disapproval at his staying home to write his thesis, while his wife worked"	"Wary of the neighbourhood" "European migrants" (i.e. *not* Australians)	n.a.
Interpretation:	➢ Do not accept that the couple does not follow traditional roles and a traditional workday. Are very traditional themselves.	➢ Do not feel that they belong as Australians into this neighbourhood, are unfamiliar with other ways of life.	➢ Only character that does not appear to judge the others.
Quotation:		"Watched in disgust as the little boy next door urinated in the street", "The child's head was shaved regularly, he assumed, in order to make his hair grow thick."	
Interpretation:		➢ Do not understand the customs and educational principles that the Macedonians follow.	
Quotation:		The young husband [...] suspected that the widower was deliberately antagonising them.	
Interpretation:		➢ Reacts with aggression that worsens because he is unable to ask the widower in person about his reasons for working at unsuitable times on something seemingly useless. • Appear to be the most prejudiced	

Handlungsverlauf

Die Schülerinnen und Schüler teilen sich in Kleingruppen auf und setzen sich mit dem Handlungsverlauf der Geschichte nach dem Prinzip einer Fallstudie auseinander. Es werden in der Gruppe ein Helfer und ein Schriftführer bestimmt, der Rest der Gruppe setzt sich mit dem Arbeitsauftrag auseinander. Diese Form der Gruppenarbeit soll zum einen den Schülerinnen und Schülern helfen, Fakten zu analysieren, zum anderen kann so ein Konsens entwickelt werden.

Je nach Zusammensetzung der Lerngruppe kann eine grobe Struktur vorgegeben werden, die Sicherung soll durch eine Folie/ein Tafelbild am Ende erfolgen, bei dem alle Ergebnisse zusammengetragen werden.

Reread the story and concentrate on its chronological development. The events described happen over the course of one year; describe how the neighbourhood develops into a community.

Lösungsvorschlag:

Summer:
- Couple moves in.
- Young man and woman feel uncomfortable.

↓

- "Relations were uncomfortable for many months."
  – Hardly any communication between the neighbours

↓

Autumn:
- Couple starts gardening; neighbours offer advice; young man takes their advice although he resents this; young woman is kind to the child; Macedonian woman gives them garlic cloves to plant.
- Couple build a hen-house; Polish widower rebuilds it without permission when it falls down; couple can't understand Polish.

↓

- Macedonian neighbours take the first step in helping the couple; the young man still resents this, but his wife reacts to the kindness.
- Polish neighbour takes the second step in helping without being asked.
  – The relationships gradually develop in small steps; initiative stems from the European migrants.

↓

Winter:
- Couple finds "themselves smiling back at the neighbours" and exchanges gifts with them (cabbage, grappa, firewood).
- Couple gains self-confidence about their living situation and defend it against criticism by the parents.

↓

- The young couple still appears cautious and only reacts to the small gestures of kindness, but they seem to start identifying with them.
  - The relationship gradually improves.

↓

Spring:
- Macedonian family shows the couple how to slaughter their ducks; they all do it together and have conversations despite the language barriers.
- Young woman becomes pregnant.

↓

- The couple still remains passive, but the migrants involve themselves in their lives.
  - The neighbours develop a sense of community.

↓

Late spring:
- Polish widower begins to build something; couple is angry about the noise.
- Whole neighbourhood knows of the pregnancy; give them small presents, are friendly and smile.

↓

- The young man still has trouble accepting the Polish widower's lifestyle.
  - The pregnancy is a key factor in the development from a neighbourhood into a community.

↓

Late summer:
- Polish widower has almost finished a two-car garage; young man is angry about this.
- Polish man gives him firewood.
- Young woman gives birth to a boy; the young man shows emotions at the neighbours' kindness.

↓

– The neighbourhood has developed into a community.

4.2 What does it mean to be Australian? The quest for national identity

Der abschließende Text des australischen Soziologen Hugh Mackay (***Copy 27***) fasst die wesentlichen Aspekte der Unterrichtsreihe noch einmal zusammen und bietet aufgrund der teilweise provokanten Aussagen und Perspektiven ausreichende Sprechanlässe für eine abschließende Debatte mit den Schülerinnen und Schülern, in denen zentrale Elemente der Unterrichtsreihe noch einmal aufgegriffen werden können.

Read the text and gather together the most important aspects Mackay mentions. Think about whether you agree or not and note down your thoughts.

Mögliches Tafelbild:

Mackay: National identity
• He doesn't consider this question to be too important: "I hope you haven't lost any sleep over Australia's [...] sense of identity".
• The question of national identity often results in "offensive stereotypes".
• He is radical in asking to "forget all about it".
• He believes in the Australian people on the whole: "we're all here and we all count".

Zur Vorbereitung der Debatte kann den Schülerinnen und Schülern ***Copy 26*** dienen, in der die wesentlichen Regeln einer *debate* im britischen *House of Parliament* beschrieben werden. Die Schülerinnen und Schüler sollen diese Regeln während der Debatte angemessen berücksichtigen. Durch eindeutige Rollenzuordnung soll zugleich sichergestellt werden, dass sich alle Schülerinnen und Schüler angemessen beteiligen.

A debate

Holding a debate:
All students are divided into proposers and opposers. Seven students take the following roles:

- Speaker. This person chairs the debate but cannot take part or vote.
- First proposer
- First opposer
- Opposer to sum up
- Proposer to sum up
- Two tellers to count the votes

Rules:

- The speaker chairs the debate.
- Everyone can only speak once during the debate and the speech should be about two minutes long.
- It's possible to 'intervene', e.g. to ask a question about a point being made.
- If someone wants to speak during the debate, s/he should catch the speaker's eye by standing up as soon as someone has finished speaking.
- If someone is spotted breaking these rules, the speaker has to be informed. This is called a point of order.

Order:

1. The speaker presents the motion.
2. First proposer presents the arguments.
3. First opposer presents the arguments against the motion.
4. A proposer presents arguments for the motion.
5. An opposer presents arguments against the motion.
6. This continues until everyone has had her/his say.
7. An opposer sums up their group's main argument.
8. A proposer sums up their group's main argument.
9. One side of the classroom is named the 'aye' wall and the opposite side the 'no' wall.
10. The speaker re-reads the motion.

Vote:

1. Everyone votes to support or oppose the motion. They do so by going to the 'aye' or 'no' side of the classroom. The speaker can't vote.
2. The tellers count up the votes on either side of the room.
3. The result of the vote is announced by speaker.

http://news.bbc.co.uk/cbbcnews/hi/newsid_4450000/newsid_4458000/4458081.stm [08.12.10] (adapted)

Hugh Mackay: Wave away any notion of identity (2002)

I hope you haven't lost any sleep over Australia's – or your own – sense of identity. As Pierre Ryckmans once put it: 'The search for a sense of identity is like the quest for happiness: if you seek it, you'll never find it.'

One of the marks of our national immaturity is the hand-wringing that goes on, from time to time, about 'what it means to be an Australian', about whether Australia has managed to create a unique place in some imagined mosaic of identities of the nations of the world. Most of those alleged 'identities' amount to little more than offensive stereotypes – the mean Scots, the mad Irish, the meticulous Swiss, the passionate Italians, the boring Swedes, the relentless Germans, the sentimental Americans, the whingeing Poms.

How would we fare on a list like that? We might wish others would praise our tolerance, our harmonious and egalitarian society, our willingness to help each other out in a crisis, our fighting qualities, our resourcefulness, our rule of law, our stable institutions. But national stereotypes are rarely kind: we might find we're being caricatures for our racism, our triumphal, our reflexive obeisance to the United States, the chip on our shoulder, our tall poppy syndrome, our harsh treatment of refugees ... or even our ugly reputation for sledging on the sporting field.

The truth about us is the truth about all human societies: we are a complex and self-contradictory mixture of all the factors – attractive and unattractive – that makes humans such a fascinating and infuriating species. [...]

The arsonists who light bushfires are Australians, as much a part of who we are as the fire-fighters who risk their lives on our behalf.

The place teems with volunteers who do everything from raising money for hospitals to foster-parenting troubled kids to working on aid projects. It also teems with self-absorbed prats who wouldn't recognise a charitable act if it hit them in the heart. We have a booming market in illicit drugs, yet a crime rate the envy of most countries. We probably worry about the degeneration of Australian society more than is justified, though there are grounds for a bit of worry. Who isn't extra vigilant? Who leaves the house unlocked?

We have a thriving arts culture that nurtures some brilliant writers, artists, composers and performers. And we've lost others who felt alienated by a strong anti-intellectual and anti-cultural stream in Australian life. Some of our leaders in politics, business and the professions think sport is the pinnacle of Aussie culture and the only real heroes are sporting heroes; others work tirelessly to support the arts.

Australia has been built on immigration but we continue to resist – as we always have – the latest wave of arrivals, and to attribute every imaginable social ill to their pernicious influence. We are torn between wanting to close the door, right now, and digest what we have, and also wanting to increase the flood of new blood, new ideas, new energy. Some of us bleat out the failure of migrants to learn English, while others are patiently teaching them, year after year, to do just that. [...]

National identity? You've got to be joking. My advice, for what it's worth, is to forget all about it. In another hundred years, we might have a better idea of what we're becoming but, even then, I suspect the answer will be too complicated to mean much.

Paradoxical though it might seem, cultural integration proceeds in tandem with cultural fragmentation. We divide, unite, separate and combine, variously and continuously. That's how we grow, evolve a perpetually unfinished quilt, we are both many and one, but 'one' is neither monocultural nor static.

The main thing about us is that we're all here and we all count. Isn't that enough to be going with?

from: P. Goldworthy (Ed.) (2008), *True Blue – On being Australia*, Allan & Unwin

Anhang

Weiterführende Literatur

- Beasley, Jack (1964): *The Rage for Life: the Work of Katharine Susannah Prichard*, Sydney: Current Book Distributors.
- Bennett, Bruce (2002): *Australian Short Fiction*, St. Lucia, Queensland: University of Queensland Press.
- Czajkowski, Bernice/Richard McRoberts (2000): *A Student's Guide to Going Home by Archie Weller*, Ballarat: Wizard Books.
- Denoghue, J./Trauter, B. (2003): *Convict Ancestry: A Neglected Aspect of Australian Identity.* In: Nations and Nationalism 9/4, pp. 555–577.
- Edelson, Phyllis F. (1993): *Australian Literature. An Anthology of Writing from the Land Down Under*, New York: Ballantine.
- Goldsworthy, Peter (Hrsg.) (2008): *True Blue. On Being Australian*, New South Wales: Allen & Unwin.
- Healy, John J. (1989): *Literature and the Aborigine in Australia*, St Lucia: University of Queensland Press.
- Hirst, J.B. (1983): *Convict Society and its Enemies. A History of Early New South Wales*, Sydney: Allen and Unwin.
- Huggan, Graham (2007): *Australian Literature. Postcolonialism, Racism, Transnationalism*, Oxford: University Press.
- Hughes, Robert (2003): *The Fatal Shore*, London: Vintage.
- Jose, Nicholas (2009): *The Literature of Australia*, New York: Norton.
- Lawson, Henry (2001): *Selected Stories*, Sydney: HarperCollins.
- Prichard, Katharine S. (1967): *Happiness. Selected Stories by Katharine Susannah Prichard*, Sydney: Angus and Roberson.
- Shoemaker, Adam (1988): *Fiction or Assumed Fiction: The Short Stories Of Colin Johnson, Jack Davis and Archie Weller*, Connections: Aboriginal Studies Press.
- Warung, Price (1892): *Tales of the Convict System*, Sydney: The Bulletin.
- Webby, Elizabeth (2000): *Australian Literature*, Cambridge: Cambridge University Press.
- Weller, Archie (1986): *Going Home – Stories by Archie Weller*, Crows Nest, NSW: Allen & Unwin.
- Winton, Tim (1985): *Scission*, Ringwood, Victoria: Penguin.

Internetadressen

- Linksammlung Australia:
  http://www.virtualteacher.com.au/australia.html
- Australian identity (video animation):
  http://vids.myspace.com/index.cfm?fuseaction=vids.individual&videoid=46193760
- bringing-them-home-online:
  http://www.nla.gov.au/digicoll/bringing-them-home-online.html
- Aboriginal Australia Art Culture:
  http://www.aboriginalaustralia.com/
- AIATSIS:
  http://www.aiatsis.gov.au/

- Apology to Australia's Indigenous Peoples:
  http://www.nsdc.org.au/home/index.php?option=com_content&view=category&layout=blog&id=23&Itemid=64
- Australian identity – St James Ethics Centre:
  http://www.ethics.org.au/ethics-articles/australian-identity
- Australian Human Rights Commission:
  http://www.hreoc.gov.au/social_justice/statistics/index.html
- Breeding out the colour:
  http://www.stolengenerations.info/index.php?option=com_content&view=article&id=140&Itemid=109
- Convict history:
  http://www.cultureandrecreation.gov.au/articles/convicts/
  http://www.australianhistory.org/convicts.php
  http://convicthistory.com
- Convict life:
  www.convictcreations.com
  www.pilotguides.com/destination_guide/pacific/australia/convict_australia
- Life in the Outback (Video)
  http://australianetwork.com/life/outback.htm
- Marcus Clarke – *For the Term of his Natural Life* (E-Book):
  http://ebooks.adelaide.edu.au/c/clarke/marcus/c59f/
- Multicultural Australia:
  www.multiculturalaustralia.edu.au
- Rabbit-Proof Fence (excerpts and viewing activities)
  http://citizen-global.wikispaces.com/Rabbit+Proof+Fence
  http://aso.gov.au/titles/features/rabbit-proof-fence/clip1/
- Australia's cultural diversity:
  http://www.racismnoway.com.au/library/cultural/index-Diversit-2.html
- The Stolen Generations – European Network for Indigenous Australian Rights:
  http://www.eniar.org/stolengenerations.html

Didaktische Literatur

- Brüning, L./Saum, T. (2009): *Erfolgreich unterrichten durch Kooperatives Lernen. Strategien zur Schüleraktivierung*, Bd. 1: Essen: Neue Deutsche Schule.
- Grieser-Kindel, C./Henseler, R./Möller, S. (2009): *Method Guide. Methoden für einen kooperativen und individualisierenden Englischunterricht in den Klassen 5–12*. Paderborn: Schöningh.
- Thaler, E. (2009): *Method Guide. Kreative Methoden für den Literaturunterricht in den Klassen 7–12*. Paderborn: Schöningh.

Bildquellenverzeichnis

S. 29: National Library of Australia – **S. 30:** State Library of Victoria, Queensland – **S. 32:** taken from *The fell tyrant or the suffering convict* by William Ross, London, 1836 – **S. 47:** National Gallery of Australia, Canberra – **S. 68:** Parliament of Australia – **S. 72:** © AP Photo/ Rob Griffith

Sollte trotz aller Bemühungen um korrekte Urheberangaben ein Irrtum unterlaufen sein, bitten wir darum, sich mit dem Verlag in Verbindung zu setzen, damit wir eventuell erforderliche Korrekturen vornehmen können.

EinFach Englisch
Unterrichtsmodelle

Herausgegeben von Hans Kröger

Ausgewählte Titel der Reihe:

Bend it Like Beckham
Filmanalyse
86 S., DIN A4, geh. Best.-Nr. 041212

Cultures in Conflict?
Literature on Ethnic Relationships
115 S., DIN A4, kart. Best.-Nr. 041220
Audio-CD: ca. 74 Min. Best.-Nr. 062407
Textausgabe: 148 S. Best.-Nr. 041218

Dead Poets Society
Filmanalyse
67 S., DIN A4, geh. Best.-Nr. 041255

East is East
Filmanalyse
102 S., DIN A4, geh. Best.-Nr. 041228

Echoes of the Empire. The Mixed Voices of a Colonial Past
20th Century English Short Stories
119 S., DIN A4, kart. Best.-Nr. 041223
Audio-CD: 78 Min. Best.-Nr. 062405
Textausgabe: 168 S. Best.-Nr. 041224

Forrest Gump
Filmanalyse
66 S., DIN A4, geh. Best.-Nr. 041231

Fried Green Tomatoes
Filmanalyse
136 S., DIN A4, kart. Best.-Nr. 041244

Political Speeches
Historical & Topical Issues
127 S., DIN A4, kart. Best.-Nr. 041236
Audio-CD: 70 Min. Best.-Nr. 062409
Textausgabe: 132 S. Best.-Nr. 041234

Rabbit-Proof Fence
Filmanalyse
54 S., DIN A4, geh. Best.-Nr. 041240

Tennessee Williams: A Streetcar Named Desire
102 S., DIN A4, geh. Best.-Nr. 041238
Textausgabe: 109 S. Best.-Nr. 041192

Strange Fruit and Other Songs
Cries for Social Consciousness and Civil Rights
59 S., mit Audio-CD,
DIN A4, geh. Best.-Nr. 041246

Urban Poetry
84 S., DIN A4, geh. Best.-Nr. 041232
Audio-CD: ca. 25 Min. Best.-Nr. 062413

Utopia and Dystopia
Exploring Alternative Worlds
92 S., DIN A4, kart. Best.-Nr. 041204
Textausgabe: 92 S. Best.-Nr. 041202

Paul Auster: Moon Palace
76 S., DIN A4, geh. Best.-Nr. 041226

Ray Bradbury: Fahrenheit 451
72 S., DIN A4, geh. Best.-Nr. 041214

Mark Haddon: The Curious Incident of the Dog in the Night-Time
99 S., DIN A4, kart. Best.-Nr. 041252

Lorraine Hansberry: A Raisin in the Sun
98 S., DIN A4, kart. Best.-Nr. 041241

Nick Hornby: About a Boy
inkl. Filmanalyse
93 S., DIN A4, kart. Best.-Nr. 041245

Aldous Huxley: Brave New World
93 S., DIN A4, kart. Best.-Nr. 041249

Ruth Prawer Jhabvala: Heat and Dust
87 S., DIN A4, geh. Best.-Nr. 041199

Harper Lee: To Kill a Mockingbird
108 S., DIN A4, kart. Best.-Nr. 041213

Ian McEwan: The Cement Garden
55 S., DIN A4, geh. Best.-Nr. 041251

Joyce Carol Oates: Big Mouth & Ugly Girl
84 S., DIN A4, geh. Best.-Nr. 041233

Meg Rosoff: How I Live Now
106 S., DIN A4, kart. Best.-Nr. 041253

Challenges – Global learning in a globalised world

Modelle und Methoden für den Englischunterricht

Herausgegeben von Engelbert Thaler

America's Global Role – Leader or Loner?
Von Iris Edelbrock und Andrea Schulz
78 S., 978-3-14-040206-4

Global Conflicts – Political Solutions
Von Martin Kohn
54 S., 978-3-14-040203-3

Global Warming – Earth's Climate at the Tipping Point?
Von Katharina Einhoff
62 S., 978-3-14-040201-9

The Changing Face of Multicultural Britain
Von Antje Blume
62 S., 978-3-14-040202-6

Popular Culture – Football, Films and Fashion
Von Engelbert Thaler
52 S., 978-3-14-040211-8

Science (Fiction) in the Third Millennium
Von Kirsten Pottbäcker
62 S., 978-3-14-040207-1

Terrorism – A Global Threat?
Von Patricia Anslinger und Gisa van Els
62 S., 978-3-14-040200-2

Global Economy – Hype, Hazard or Hope?
Von Iris Edelbrock und Birgit Schmidt-Grob
70 S., mit vierfarb. OH-Folien, 978-3-14-040209-5

Advertising and Marketing – Products, Promises and Persuasion
Von Iris Edelbrock und Birgit Schmidt-Grob
54 S., mit vierfarb. OH-Folien, 978-3-14-040210-1

Gender Matters – Exploring Male-Female Relationships
Von Engelbert Thaler
62 S., 978-3-14-040208-8

Them and Us – On the Way to One World?
Von Katrin Kollmeyer
62 S., 978-3-14-040205-7

Source of Conflict or Recipe for Peace? – Religion in a Globalised World
Von Ulrich Schnakenberg
62 S., 978-3-14-040204-0

Weitere Titel sind in Vorbereitung.

Schöningh Verlag
Postfach 2540
33055 Paderborn

Schöningh

Fordern Sie unseren Prospekt zur kompletten Reihe an:
Informationen 0800 / 18 18 787 (freecall)
info@schoeningh.de / www.schoeningh-schulbuch.de